Companions in the Mission of Jesus

Texts for Prayer and Reflection
in the Lenten and Easter Seasons

Georgetown University Press
for
The New York Province of
the Society of Jesus
1987

ACKNOWLEDGMENTS

Cover: Tintoretto (Jacopo Robusti, 1518–1594), *Christ by the Sea of Tiberias*: National Gallery of Art, Samuel H. Kress Collection. This representation of the appearance of the risen Jesus to seven disciples, drawn from John 21:1–8, is thought to have been painted by Tintoretto in Venice between 1575 and 1580, some twenty years after the death of St. Ignatius.

Permission from the publishers of the following copyrighted material is gratefully acknowledged:

Centrum Ignatianum Spiritualitatis, Rome, for *The Spiritual Journal of St. Ignatius Loyola*, tr. William J. Young.

Permission to quote from *The Constitutions of the Society of Jesus*, the three volumes of Selected Letters and Addresses of Pedro Arrupe, S.J., and individual volumes of Studies in the Spirituality of Jesuits was granted by the copyright holder, the Institute of Jesuit Sources, 3700 West Pine Blvd., St. Louis, Mo., 63108.

Loyola University Press, Chicago, for passages from *The Letters of St. Ignatius Loyola*, translated by William J. Young, S.J.

ISBN 0-87840-450-3

Preface

Efforts to reaffirm and strengthen our Jesuit identity have been an integral part of our Renewal and Planning Program over the past two years. Our province-wide experience of the Spiritual Exercises in Daily Life last year proved to be a truly graced moment in the history of the province. So much so that many of the small group reports at last June's Province Conference recommended that we continue to pray together as a province this year, even as we move into the more concrete aspects of planning for the future.

In response to these recommendations, the Province Planning Committee, with my encouragement, commissioned the publication of this book. I am confident that it will serve us well as an instrument to deepen our apostolic prayer and Jesuit roots.

I am grateful for the leadership of the Planning Committee in responding to the recommendations made at the Province Conference. Special thanks to Fr. Brian E. Daley and Fr. Vincent T. O'Keefe, who conceived the scheme of the book and chose the texts; and to Fr. John B. Breslin and Ms. Deborah McCann of the Georgetown University Press, who fashioned the design of the book and saw it through to production.

Joseph A. Novak, S.J.
Provincial
New York Province

COMPANIONS IN THE MISSION OF JESUS

Contents

Foreword

The aim of the renewal and planning throughout the Society of Jesus is to establish the future orientations to which the Spirit is calling us in and for the Church. It is a process that must follow the unchanging apostolic demands of our Ignatian charism and spirit, and it is in answer to the challenges put to us by the Church and by the society we live in.

St. Ignatius founded our Society as a company of men who would continuously renew themselves through the inner vigor of his *Spiritual Exercises* and the vitalizing impulse of the Spirit. And thus we would move to accomplish those things which our vocation and mission to promote God's greater glory and the service of the human family demand in any given age. Renewal and planning, therefore, are signs of life and vitality as we follow our Ignatian charism and respond to the inspiration of the Spirit.

In their programs for renewal and planning, many Provinces devoted an initial period to making the Spiritual Exercises in Daily Life. This was clearly the first step to take since the *Spiritual Exercises* are the inner dynamism of our life and mission, the wellspring of our apostolate. They enable us to renew our faith and apostolic hope by experiencing again the love of God in Jesus Christ. They enable us to renew and strengthen our commitment to be companions of Jesus in his mission, to be "placed with the Son." They help us to attain the freedom of mind and heart that we need for renewal and planning as a Jesuit process, to be ready for whatever the Lord will ask of us.

The *Spiritual Exercises* are the fundamental experience which gave birth to our Society, starting with the first group of companions who offered themselves to Paul III, desiring to be called the Company of Jesus, and asking to be sent to any part of the world where there was hope of greater service of God and greater help for men and women.

The Society had to set down some common terms of reference to capture this spirit of the *Spiritual Exercises*. This was done from the beginning with the "Formula of the Institute" and the *Constitutions*. In a sense, the Society received its life in the *Spiritual Exercises* and its formulation in the *Constitutions*, which are the crystallization of an experience that was religious, personal and communitarian, an experience of God and of his Gospel as lived by the first Companions of Jesus. It must never be forgotten that the *Constitutions* are to be understood as the concrete application of the spirit of the *Spiritual Exercises* to the exigencies of an apostolic order that is flexible and available for the service of the Church and the human family.

The Second Vatican Council spoke clearly and forcefully about this very point by launching a program of adaptation and renewal for all religious institutes. It indicated the path to be followed by setting out a double objective to guide this program: a return to the sources of the religious institute's particular charism; and, at the same time, an adaptation to the changed conditions of the times.

Our last three General Congregations centered their attention and hopes on applying the spirit and teaching of Vatican II to the life and mission and work of our Society. Certain key elements were indicated for us in our renewed life and apostolic planning: adaptation and renewal in relation to the changed and changing conditions of the times; a full and free consultation of the members; and a continuous recall that our life is inseparably religious and apostolic.

Our former Superior General, Father Pedro Arrupe, and our present one, Father Peter-Hans Kolvenbach, have worked strenuously at their mandate from the last three General Congregations to clarify and promote the program of renewal and planning to be undertaken throughout our Society. They have called our prayerful and continual attention to addresses and letters of the present Holy Father, John Paul II, and of his immediate predecessors, John Paul I and Paul VI, as vital for our service of the church.

It is in accord with the dynamic of a Jesuit process of renewal and planning that the present book turns to a selection of passages: from the "Formula of the Institute," and the *Constitutions*, as well as the letters of St. Ignatius; from addresses and writings of the recent Popes; from our last three General Congregations; and from the writings of Father Arrupe and Father Kolvenbach. General Congregation XXXIII provides us with a clear orientation in this sense: "In recent years a renewed consciousness concerning our religious life has been felt throughout the Society. The decrees of GC XXXI (8, 13–17, 19) and GC XXXII (2, 4, 11), as well as the writings of Father Arrupe, have developed a spiritual doctrine at once profoundly rooted in the Gospel and our tradition and yet one which responds to the challenges of our times" (n.10).

As companions of Jesus and as friends in the Lord who ask to be placed with the Son, may we hear again his call and invitation: come with me, toil with me, be by my side in suffering and in glory.

Vincent T. O'Keefe, S.J.

Introduction

This book of texts has been compiled to provide stimulation and support for Jesuits who are reflecting prayerfully on their corporate identity, and who are trying to gain a more acute sense of what that identity should mean for the Church of today and tomorrow.

Many of us, in various American Provinces of the Society of Jesus, have made the "Spiritual Exercises in Daily Life," with the help of the guide published last year by the Maryland Province, *Place Me With Your Son*. This book is meant as a sequel and companion to that volume, in the hope that it will nourish our continued prayer in the spirit of the *Exercises*. It is an anthology of passages taken from the writings of St. Ignatius and our foundation documents, from the documents of the last three General Congregations, and from the letters and addresses of recent Popes and Fathers General, arranged thematically in such a way as to be suitable for prayerful reading during the Lenten and Easter seasons. The passages have been chosen to provide possible material for personal meditative prayer each day, as well as for continuing spiritual conversation within our Jesuit communities.

Clearly there are many ways in which one might select and arrange texts in a collection such as this. We have taken as our inspiration and structural guide the title and content of the main document of G.C. 33: *Companions of Jesus Sent into Today's World*. This seemed not only an apposite and timely summary of what the Society of Jesus, in the most general terms, understands itself to be, but also to be strikingly parallel to the liturgical and spiritual dynamics of the Paschal season.

Lent, after all, invites us each year to become disciples of Jesus once again: to hear his urgent call to conversion of heart

1

and to follow him on his way—a way of companionship that leads, in Holy Week, to a personal and sacramental immersion in the Paschal Mystery. Easter then calls us to be not only disciples but apostles: it reminds us that the news of Jesus' resurrection is not only a cause for joy and hope, but a commission to preach this news to all people, a summons to become a Church of disciples and to labor that that Church might become incarnate in every time and place, among those who are ready for God's Kingdom. So the news that Jesus is risen, that he lives and speaks in our midst, leads inevitably to the transforming experience of Pentecost, and to our consciousness of being a community shaped and led by the Spirit of the risen Lord.

Corresponding to this liturgical progression from discipleship to apostleship, from walking with Jesus to being sent out by him as his heralds, we have here selected texts for Lent that focus our attention on aspects of our companionship with Jesus and with each other, and for the Easter season passages that concentrate on ministry and mission. In a sense, such a division is inappropriate for Jesuits: as our documents continually remind us, our companionship with each other and with the Lord —our life as religious, as contemplatives—is only realized genuinely "in action," by our sharing in his mission from the Father. We already live wholly within the power of Easter. Even so, it seems to be both liturgically and practically appropriate to continue our personal and corporate renewal by reflecting, during Lent, on what we are called to *be*, in Christ—on what it means, for a Jesuit, to be "conformed" by God "to the image of his Son" (Rom. 8.29)—and then to contemplate, in the spirit of Easter and Pentecost, the practical implications of this conformity for our action—for what we are called, in the Spirit of Jesus, to *do*.

Our collection begins, then, with several passages that remind us of our need for conversion of heart, if we are to be true disciples of Jesus: preliminary considerations for the days between Ash Wednesday and the First Sunday of Lent. During the First Week of Lent, the focus is on Jesuit life as a life led in companionship, since that is the original and characteristic model for our existence as a religious body. We turn then, in the Second Week of Lent, to consider the role of prayer—personal companionship with Jesus and personal sharing in his role as Son—as the heart of our companionship with each other. During the following three weeks, we present texts that treat of our three religious vows, as they give form to our desire to follow Christ together: chastity, and the particular kind of affective life it is meant to engender (Third Week of Lent); poverty, as the material setting for our common life and ministry (Fourth Week of Lent); obedience, as the prime strategy for uniting us with God and incorporating us into his plan of salvation (Fifth Week of Lent). In Holy Week, as the Church tries to follow Jesus on the way of his Passion, we offer texts that remind us of our fundamental desire, formed in the *Exercises* and nourished by our Eucharistic fellowship, to make that way peculiarly our own.

With Easter, as I have said, the emphasis of our anthology shifts from companionship to mission. During Easter Week, the texts we have chosen are meant to remind us of the central apostolic or missionary identity of the Society of Jesus. In those offered for the Second Week of Easter, that mission can be seen more specifically as the task of building up the universal Church, concretely realized in ecclesial communion with the Bishop of Rome. During the Third Week of Easter, our texts remind us of the historic implications of that ecclesial commitment for the Society, in terms of our universal pastoral concern—expressed in the fourth vow of the professed—and of our ideals of mobility and apostolic availability. Next, in the Fourth and Fifth Weeks of Easter, we present passages that remind us of two special emphases the contemporary Society has chosen to make in defining our mission more concretely for today: the linking of our preaching of the Gospel with the promotion of justice (Fourth Week), and the preference of poor people as our companions and as the objects of our ministry (Fifth Week). In the Sixth Week of Easter, texts have been cho-

4

sen to help us contemplate some of the main ways in which the Society's mission has been realized through our history: the sacramental and pastoral work of "reformed priests," the effort to resist atheism, the ministries of education, communication and social work—all carried out in a spirit of collaboration with our fellow disciples, whether they are lay or clerical, men or women. For the Seventh Week of Easter, finally, we have selected texts that will turn our attention to the constant need we share, as Jesuits, to evaluate and redirect our apostolic ministries, and to discern the way in which the Spirit of the risen Lord—the Spirit poured out once at Pentecost, and given abundantly also to us—may be leading us in the days ahead.

After each week's collection of texts, we have suggested a few further books or documents that pertain to the theme of that week. We have also suggested some books for general or background reading at the beginning of the anthology. These are not meant to be exhaustive bibliographies of the available literature on Jesuit life and renewal, but simply lists of further readings in English that can flesh out or place in context the themes touched on in this collection, and that should be easily available in most of our community libraries.

Each of us, undoubtedly, could make his own anthology of favorite passages that sum up, for him, the challenge and the consolation of Jesuit life. This collection is surely not definitive in any sense; it is meant simply to represent some of the central ideals of our tradition, and to invite all of us to pray and think and speak together on the things that matter most to us, nourished from the abundant depths of our own wells. It is our hope that this anthology, however individual Jesuits and groups within our communities choose to use it, will help us all towards a deeper understanding of our vocation, towards a renewal of our commitment to life in the Lord's company, and towards growing clarity about the direction in which he wants to shape our future.

Brian E. Daley, S.J.
Advent, 1986

Abbreviations

The following abbreviations are used in this collection of texts:

Apostolates: Pedro Arrupe, S.J., *Other Apostolates Today* (Selected Letters and Addresses, 3: ed. Jerome Aixalá, S.J.; St. Louis, 1981).

Challenge: Pedro Arrupe, S.J., *Challenge to Religious Life Today* (Selected Letters and Addresses, 1: ed. Jerome Aixalá, S.J.; St. Louis, 1979).

CIS: Publications of the *Centrum Ignatianum Spiritualitatis*, Rome.

Ganss: St. Ignatius of Loyola, *The Constitutions of the Society of Jesus*, translated, with introduction and commentary, by George E. Ganss, S.J. (St. Louis, 1970).

Justice: Pedro Arrupe, S.J., *Justice with Faith Today* (Selected Letters and Addresses, 2: ed. Jerome Aixalá, S.J.; St. Louis, 1980).

Legacy: *The Spiritual Legacy of Pedro Arrupe, S.J.* (Letters and Addresses of Pedro Arrupe, S.J., and Peter-Hans Kolvenbach, S.J.; New York, 1985).

Planet: Pedro Arrupe, S.J., *A Planet to Heal: Reflections and Forecasts* (Letters and Addresses: ed. John Harriott, S.J.; Rome, 1975).

Studies: Studies in the Spirituality of Jesuits (The American Assistancy Seminar on Jesuit Spirituality; St. Louis, 1969–).

Young: *The Letters of St. Ignatius of Loyola*, translated by William J. Young, S.J. (Chicago, 1959).

Recommended for General and Background Reading

William V. Bangert, S.J., *A History of the Society of Jesus* (St. Louis, 1972).

Simon Decloux, S.J., *Commentaries on the Letters and Spiritual Diary of St. Ignatius Loyola* (Rome, 1980). Includes the autograph text of the *Spiritual Diary*, in the translation of William J. Young, S.J.

Cándido de Dalmases, S.J., *Ignatius of Loyola, Founder of the Jesuits. His Life and Work* (St. Louis, 1985).

Joseph de Guibert, S.J., *The Jesuits: their Spiritual Doctrine and Practice; a Historical Study* (Chicago, 1964).

Harvey D. Egan, S.J., *The Spiritual Exercises and the Ignatian Mystical Horizon* (St. Louis, 1976).

H. Outram Evenett, *The Spirit of the Counter-Reformation* (Cambridge, 1968).

John W. O'Malley, S.J., *The Jesuits, St. Ignatius and the Counter-Reformation. Some Recent Studies and their Implication for Today* (Studies XIV, 1: January, 1982).

John W. Padberg, S.J., *The General Congregations of the Society of Jesus: a Brief Survey of their History* (Studies VI, 1-2: January–March, 1974).

—, *Personal Experience and the Spiritual Exercises. The Example of St. Ignatius* (Studies X, 5: November, 1978).

—, *The Society True to Itself. A Brief History of the 32nd General Congregation of the Society of Jesus* (Studies XV, 3-4: May–September, 1983).

Hugo Rahner, S.J., *Ignatius the Theologian* (New York, 1968).

—, *The Vision of Ignatius in the Chapel at La Storta* (CIS, Recherches 6; Rome, 1975).

—, *Ignatius: the Man and the Priest* (CIS, Recherches 11; Rome, 1977).

Karl Rahner, S.J., and Paul Imhof, S.J., *Ignatius of Loyola* (London, 1979).

Joseph Tylenda, S.J., ed., *Counsels for Jesuits: Selected Letters and Instructions of St. Ignatius Loyola* (Chicago, 1986).

Friedrich Wulf, S.J., ed., *Ignatius of Loyola: his Personality and Spiritual Heritage, 1556–1956* (St. Louis, 1972).

Companions in the Mission of Jesus

I. The Preparation Days of Lent: A CALL TO CONVERSION

1. Ash Wednesday

What is it to be a Jesuit? It is to know that one is a sinner, yet called to be a companion of Jesus as Ignatius was: Ignatius, who begged the Blessed Virgin to "place him with her Son," and who then saw the Father himself ask Jesus, carrying his Cross, to take this pilgrim into his company.

(G. C. 32, 11: *Jesuits Today* [Decree 2], par. 1)

2. Thursday after Ash Wednesday

If you consider the nature of your vocation, you will see that what would not be slight in others would be slight in you. For not only has God called you out of darkness into his marvelous light, and translated you into the Kingdom of his beloved Son, as he has done with the rest of the faithful, but... he thought it good to withdraw you from the perilous sea of this world...—the desire now of possessions, now of honors, now of pleasures—and, on the other hand, from the fear of losing all such things...

It is true that all the orders in the Church are directed to this end. And yet God has called you to this, in which his glory and the salvation of the neighbor are set before you, not as a general end but one toward which all your life and its various activities must be made by you into a continuous sacrifice. This requires a cooperation from you that should not stop with example and earnest prayer, but includes all the exterior means which his divine providence has provided for the mutual help we should give one another. From this you can understand how noble and royal is the manner of life you have chosen.

(St. Ignatius Loyola, Letter to the Fathers and Scholastics at Coimbra [May 27 (?), 1547]: Young 122)

3. Friday after Ash Wednesday

If we are to hear and respond to the call of God in this kind of world, then we must have a discerning attitude. For us Jesuits the way of discernment involves: the examination of conscience, prayer and brotherly dialogue within our communities, and the openness to superiors that facilitates obedience.

We cannot attain this discerning attitude without self-abnegation. Sign of our joy at the approach of the Kingdom (Matt. 13.44) and result of a progressive identification with Christ, who "emptied himself, being born in the likeness of humanity" (Phil. 2.7), this abnegation is required by the Spiritual Exercises: to divest ourselves of "self-love, self-will and self-interest" (Spir. Ex. 189). It is only through detachment from all we have and are that we can receive all from God in faith and give ourselves wholly to others in love. Without such an attitude, we cannot present ourselves as interiorly free enough for the authentic service of him who calls us.

(G. C. 33, 13-14: *Companions of Jesus Sent into Today's World* [Decree 1], pars. 12-13)

4. Saturday after Ash Wednesday

Christianity is not a this-worldly power structure imposing itself according to a set of laws. Christianity is not a strategy that merely has to be applied according to the rules in order to be successful. Christianity is the breakthrough of God in time and in the world, a breakthrough that happened historically in Christ and continues to happen again and again in every true Christian. Humans can obstruct or prevent this breakthrough of God, and, in fact, we are very clever in finding obstacles. When this happens, the Gospel remains a dead letter, and we will be unable to hear the radical message of the Gospel because we distort it through our unbridled selfishness. We will not be capable of undertaking the necessary personal and social changes because we are afraid of the consequences this would entail for ourselves personally.

I am deeply convinced of one thing: without a profound personal conversion, we shall not be able to answer the challenge facing us today. If, however, we succeed in tearing down the barriers within ourselves, then we shall have a new experience of God breaking through, and we shall know what it means to be a Christian today.

(Pedro Arrupe, S.J., "Faith and Justice as a Task for European Christians," [Nov. 21, 1976], *Justice* 192f.)

14

Recommended for Further Reading:

St. Ignatius Loyola, *Autobiography*, chap. 1.

—, Letter to Scholastics at Coimbra (May 27 [?], 1547): Young 120–130.

G. C. 33, Decree 1: *Companions of Jesus Sent into Today's World* (esp. pars. 9–14).

R. F. Harvanek, *The Reluctance to Admit Sin* (Studies IX, 3: May, 1977).

P. Robb, *Conversion as a Human Experience* (Studies XIV, 3: May, 1982).

D. Gelpi, *The Converting Jesuit* (Studies XVIII, 1: January, 1986).

II. First Week of Lent: JESUIT COMPANIONSHIP

1. Sunday, First Week of Lent

At the meeting on the first night, the following question was opened up: given that we had offered and dedicated ourselves and our lives to Christ our Lord and to his true and legitimate vicar on earth, so that he might dispose of us and send us wherever he judged it to be more fruitful.., would it or would it not be more advantageous for our purpose to be so joined and bound together in one body that no physical distance, no matter how great, would separate us?

In the end, we established the affirmative side of the question, that is, that in as much as our most kind and affectionate Lord had deigned to gather us together and unite us, men so spiritually weak and from such diverse geographical and cultural backgrounds, we ought not split apart what God has gathered and united; on the contrary, we ought day by day to strengthen and stabilize our union, rendering ourselves one body with special concern for each other, in order to effect the greater spiritual good of our fellow men. For united spiritual strength is more robust and braver in any arduous enterprise than it would be if segmented.

(*Deliberatio Primorum Patrum* 3: *Cons MHSJ* I, 3; tr. J. J. Toner, *The Deliberation that Started the Jesuits:* Studies VI, 4 [June, 1974], 190–192)

2. Monday, First Week of Lent

The more difficult it is for the members of this congregation to be united with their head and among themselves, since they are so scattered among the faithful and among the unbelievers in diverse regions of the world, the more ought means to be sought for that union. For the Society cannot be preserved or governed, or, consequently, attain the end it seeks for the greater glory of God unless its members are united among themselves and with their head.

(*Constitutions* VIII, 1 [655]: Ganss 285)

3. *Tuesday, First Week of Lent*

The chief bond to cement the union of the members among themselves and with their head is, on both sides, the love of God our Lord. For when the superior and the subjects are closely united to his divine and supreme goodness, they will very easily be united among themselves, through that same love which will descend from the divine goodness and spread to all other people, particularly into the body of the Society.

(*Constitutions* VIII, 1 [671]: Ganss 291)

4. *Wednesday, First Week of Lent*

When community life flourishes, the whole religious life is sound. Obedience, for instance, is a very clear expression of our cooperation toward common ends, and it becomes more perfect to the extent that superiors and subjects are bound to one another in trust and service. Chastity is more safely preserved, "when there is a true brotherly love in community life between the members" (*Perfectae Caritatis* 12). Poverty, finally, means that we have made ourselves poor by surrendering ourselves and our possessions to follow the Lord (Luke 18.28). Community life aids and assists us in this surrender in a great variety of ways, and in its own unique way is the support of poverty. When the religious life is thus strengthened, unity and flexibility, universality, full personal dedication, and the freedom of the Gospels are also strengthened for the assistance of souls in every way. And this was the intention of the first companions.

(G. C. 31, 315: *Community Life and Religious Discipline* [Decree 19], par. 4)

5. Thursday, First Week of Lent

It is in companionship that the Jesuit fulfils his mission. He belongs to a community of friends in the Lord, who, like him, have asked to be received under the standard of Christ the King (*Spir. Ex.* 147).

This community is the entire body of the Society itself, no matter how widely dispersed over the face of the earth. The particular local community to which he may belong at any given moment is, for him, simply a concrete—if, here and now, a privileged—expression of this world-wide brotherhood.

The local Jesuit community is thus an apostolic community, not inward but outward looking, the focus of its concern being the service it is called upon to give men and women. It is contemplative but not monastic, for it is a *communitas ad dispersionem*. It is a community of men ready to go wherever they are sent.

A *communitas ad dispersionem*, but also a *koinonia*, a sharing of goods and life, with the Eucharist at its center: the sacrifice and sacrament of the Deed of Jesus, who loved his own to the end (John 13.1).

(G.C. 32, 25–28: *Jesuits Today* [Decree 2], pars. 15–18)

6. Friday, First Week of Lent

Let us realistically face the facts that make community building difficult today. More so today than in the past, our membership is drawn from very different social and cultural backgrounds. Moreover, the modern world places a much heavier stress on individual freedom than on the subordination of the individual to the group. Our response to these realities will be to transform them from obstacles to aids in community building. Our basic attitude toward cultural differences will be that they can enrich our union rather than threaten it. Our basic attitude toward personal freedom will be that freedom is fulfilled in the active service of love.

(G. C. 32, 214: *The Union of Minds and Hearts* [Decree 11], par. 16)

7. *Saturday, First Week of Lent*

For Ignatius, the Society, as a global community of all who have been formed into one body, has as its foundation the love that binds together the three Divine Persons. This love makes possible the continued existence, as one body, of what is a "community for dispersion"...

But how can our communities be inspired by the trinitarian model of personal plurality? The answer is easy: by love and by the mission given under obedience. Communion among us reflects the divine *koinonia*, for God wanted to bind us to himself by love, for a mission given to us, under obedience, not only as individuals, but as sharers together in an apostolic conspiration proceeding from him. The union that exists among us follows a divine pattern. The unification that the Spirit brings about in a community proceeds from that very unity which operates in the heart of the Trinity.

(Pedro Arrupe, S. J., "The Trinitarian Inspiration of the Ignatian Charism" [1980], 98f.: *Legacy* 133)

Recommended for Further Reading:

G. C. 31, Decree 19: *Community Life and Religious Discipline.*

G. C. 32, Decree 11: *Union of Minds and Hearts.*

Pedro Arrupe, S.J., "De Nostrorum Institutione in Spiritu," *Acta Romana S.J.* 15 (1967), 103–133.

J. J. Toner, S.J., *The Deliberation that Started the Jesuits. A Commentary on the Deliberatio Primorum Patrum. Newly Translated, with a Historical Introduction.* (Studies VI, 4: June, 1974).

M. J. Buckley, S.J., *Mission in Companionship: of Jesuit Community and Communion.* (Studies I, 4: September, 1979).

P. J. Henriot, S.J., J. Appleyard, S.J., J. L. Klein, S.J., *Living Together in Mission: a Symposium on Small Apostolic Communities.* (Studies XII, 2: March, 1980).

III. Second Week of Lent: JESUIT PRAYER AND UNION WITH GOD

1. Sunday, Second Week of Lent

For the preservation and development not only of the body or exterior of the Society but also of its spirit, and for the attainment of the objective it seeks, which is to aid souls to reach their ultimate and supernatural end, the means which unite the human instrument with God and so dispose it that it may be wielded dexterously by his divine hand are more effective than those which equip it in relation to men and women. Such means are, for example, goodness and virtue, and especially charity, and a pure intention of the divine service, and familiarity with God our Lord in spiritual exercises of devotion, and sincere zeal for souls for the sake of glory to him who created and redeemed them and not for any other benefit.

(*Constitutions* X, 2 [813]: Ganss 332)

2. Monday, Second Week of Lent

All should make diligent efforts to keep their intention right, not only in regard to their state of life but also in all particular details. In these they should always aim at serving and pleasing the Divine Goodness for its own sake and because of the incomparable love and benefits with which God has anticipated us, rather than for fear of punishments or hope of rewards, although they ought to draw help also from them. Further, they should often be exhorted to seek God our Lord in all things, stripping off from themselves the love of creatures to the extent that this is possible, in order to turn their love upon the Creator of them, by loving him in all creatures and all of them in him, in conformity with his holy and divine will.

(*Constitutions* III, 1 [288] 26: Ganss 165)

21

3. Tuesday, Second Week of Lent

Considering the end of our studies, the scholastics can hardly give themselves to prolonged meditations. Over and above the spiritual exercises assigned for their perfection—namely, daily Mass, an hour for vocal prayer and examen of conscience, and weekly confession and Communion—they should practice the seeking of God's presence in all things, in their conversations, their walks, in all that they see, taste, hear, understand, in all their actions, since his Divine Majesty is truly in all things by his presence, power, and essence. This kind of meditation, which finds God our Lord in all things, is easier than raising oneself to the consideration of divine truths which are more abstract and which demand something of an effort if we are to keep our attention on them. But this method is an excellent exercise to prepare us for great visitations of our Lord, even in prayers that are rather short.

(St. Ignatius Loyola, Letter to Fr. Antonio Brandão [June 1, 1551]: Young 240)

4. Wednesday, Second Week of Lent

To live his life of prayer, which in the Society is never separated from apostolic action, each of us must first deny himself so that, shedding his own personal inclinations, he may have that mind which is in Christ Jesus. For while, on the one hand, prayer brings forth abnegation, since it is God who purifies our hearts by his presence, on the other, abnegation itself prepares the way for prayer, because only the pure of heart will see God. Progress in prayer is possible for those alone who continually try to put off their misguided affections to ready themselves to receive the light and grace of God.

(G. C. 31, 219: Prayer [Decree 14], par. 8)

5. Thursday, Second Week of Lent

In seeking this union with God in Christ, we experience a difficulty peculiar to our times, and we must be prepared to meet it. The material conditions of our world—a world of sharply contrasted affluence and misery—and the spiritual climate engendered by them, tend to produce in our contemporaries an inner emptiness, a sense of the absence of God... In the meantime, we ourselves are sometimes plunged in this climate of emptiness; and so it is crucial for us somehow to regain that continual familiarity with God in both prayer and action which St. Ignatius considered absolutely essential to the very existence of our companionship.

We are thus led, inevitably, to the absolute necessity of personal prayer, both as a value in itself and as a source of energy for apostolic action. "The charity of Christ urges us to personal prayer and no human person can dispense us from that urgency." (G.C. 31, Decr. 14, par. 7) We need it for the familiarity with God which consists in finding him in all things, and all things in him.

(G. C. 32, 205f.: *Union of Minds and Hearts* [Decree 11], pars. 7–8)

6. Friday, Second Week of Lent

To preserve a proper balance among the religious, apostolic and priestly aspects of all our activities, particularly those of a markedly secular character, will only be possible if one has a living spiritual awareness that is shared with the brethren. Our faith should be especially strong when the work of evangelization seems to allow for or suggest only an implicit manifestation of that faith... But all this is unthinkable without the gift of God sought in humble prayer.

To live today, at every moment and in every mission, the life of a "contemplative in action" supposes a gift and a pedagogy of prayer that will give us the capacity for renewed "reading" of reality—of all reality—from the point of view of the Gospel and for continual confrontation of that reality with the Gospel.

(Pedro Arrupe, S. J., "Genuine Integration of the Spiritual Life and the Apostolate" [1976], 3: *Challenge* 194f.; *Legacy* 7)

7. Saturday, Second Week of Lent

Our spiritual and apostolic life is authentic if it frees us more and makes us more available, more "in the image of the Son". As Father Nadal used to say, the true prayer of the Society prepares us to carry out our vocation and job and, particularly, to seek perfect obedience according to our Institute. On the other hand, without a deep experience of God, without a deliberate personal identification with Jesus Christ in our life and apostolate, we would be incapable of the apostolic availability the Society asks of us. And this complete availability is the best offering we can make to God, the ideal disposition and context for all prayer and all apostolic work. (Hebr. 10.5f.; *Spir. Ex.* 46)

(Pedro Arrupe, S. J., "Apostolic Availability" (1977): *Challenge* 232f.; *Legacy* 14)

Recommended for Further Reading:

St. Ignatius Loyola, Letter to Fr. Antonio Brandão (June 1, 1551), Young 237–243.

G.C. 31, Decree 14: *Prayer*.

Pedro Arrupe, S. J., "Spiritual Renewal" (1971), *Planet* 125–134; *Challenge* 41–50.

—, "The Trinitarian Inspiration of the Ignatian Charism" (1980), *Legacy* 87–143.

J. F. Conwell, S.J., *Contemplation in Action: a Study in Ignatian Prayer* (Spokane, 1957).

R. Faricy, S.J., *Jesuit Community: Community of Prayer*. (Studies VIII, 4: October, 1976).

IV. Third Week of Lent: CHASTITY AND THE AFFECTIONS

1. Sunday, Third Week of Lent

What pertains to the vow of chastity does not require explanation, since it is evident how perfectly it should be preserved through the endeavor in this matter to imitate the angelic purity by the purity of the body and mind.

(*Constitutions*, VI, 1 [547] 1: Ganss 245 f.)

2. Monday, Third Week of Lent

I will ponder with great affection how much God our Lord has done for me, and how much he has given me of what he possesses, and finally, how much, as far as he can, the same Lord desires to give himself to me according to his divine decrees.

Then I will reflect upon myself, and consider, according to all reason and justice, what I ought to offer the Divine Majesty, that is, all I possess and myself with it.

(St. Ignatius Loyola, *Spiritual Exercises* 235)

3. Tuesday, Third Week of Lent

God, pouring forth his charity in our hearts through the Holy Spirit, confers upon some in the Church the gift of consecrated chastity, a sign of charity and likewise a stimulus to it, whereby they may more easily devote themselves with an undivided heart to him alone and to the service of his kingdom. Therefore, chastity "for the sake of the Kingdom of heaven" (Matt. 19.12), to which by both his example and his calling Christ invites us, and which we as religious profess, following the lead of so many saints, should, as the Church repeatedly urges and as our founder expressly declares, be "perfectly observed" by us.

(G. C. 31, 245: *Chastity in the Society of Jesus* [Decree 16], par. 1)

4. Wednesday, Third Week of Lent

Chastity vowed to God through celibacy implies and requires of us a sacrifice by which we knowingly and willingly forego entrance into that family relationship wherein husband and wife, parents and children, can in many ways, even psychologically, attain mutual fulfilment. Hence, our consecration to Christ involves a certain affective renunciation and a solitude of heart which form part of the cross offered to us by Jesus as we follow his footsteps, and which closely associate us with his paschal mystery and render us sharers of the spiritual fertility which flows from it. The vow of chastity, then, on the indispensable condition that it be accepted with a humble, joyous, and firm spirit as a gift from God, and be offered as a sacrifice to God, not only does not diminish our personality nor hamper human contacts and dialogue, but rather expands affectively, unites people as sisters and brothers, and brings them to a fuller charity.

(G. C. 31, 249: *Chastity in the Society of Jesus* [Decree 16], par. 6)

5. Thursday, Third Week of Lent

All should keep in mind that love consecrated by chastity should constantly grow, and approach the mature measure of the fullness of Christ (Eph. 4.13). It is, consequently, not a gift bestowed once and for all, mature and complete, at the beginning of one's spiritual life, but such as by repeated decisions, perhaps serious ones, should steadily increase and become more perfect. Thus the heart is more and more cleansed of affections not yet sufficiently understood, until the person adheres totally to Christ through love.

Such love of Jesus our Lord impels a person likewise to genuine human love for others and to true friendship. For chastity for the sake of the Kingdom of heaven is safeguarded by fraternal friendship, and in turn flowers forth in it. Hence also, we should regard as the precious apostolic fruit of ever more perfect love of friendship that mature, simple, anxiety-free dealing with the men and women with whom and for whom we exercise our ministry for the building up of the body of Christ.

(G. C. 31, 255f.: *Chastity in the Society of Jesus* [Decree 16], par. 8b)

6. Friday, Third Week of Lent

Celibacy for the sake of the Kingdom has a special apostolic value in our time, when men and women tend to put whole classes of their fellow human beings beyond the margins of their concern, while at the same time identifying love with eroticism. In such a time, the self-denying love which is warmly human, yet freely given in service to all, can be a powerful sign leading men and women to Christ, who came to show us what love really is: that God is love.

(G. C. 32, 225: *The Union of Minds and Hearts* [Decree 11], par. 26)

7. Saturday, Third Week of Lent

The *Exercises* are, in the last analysis, a method in the pedagogy of love—the pedagogy, that is, of the most pure charity towards God and towards one's neighbor. They root out of the human heart carnal and worldly love, thus opening it to the beams of God's love. A demanding love it is, calling forth in us a response of love and of service. Service, which is itself love. This is the message of the very last paragraph of the book of the *Exercises:* "The zealous service of God our Lord, out of pure love, should be esteemed above all" (*Spir. Ex.* 370). In the *Exercises*, we find terms and concepts which are logically reducible to one another: "the glory of God", for example, can be replaced by "the service of God". The same may be said of "praise" and "reverence". Only one term is final and irreducible to any other: love.

(Pedro Arrupe, S. J., "Rooted and Grounded in Love" [1981]: *Legacy* 151f.)

Recommended for Further Reading:

G. C. 31, Decree 16: *Chastity in the Society of Jesus.*

Pedro Arrupe, S. J., "Rooted and Grounded in Love" (1981), *Legacy* 145–195.

W. A. Barry, S.J., M. Birmingham, R.S.C., W. J.Connolly, S.J., R. J. Fahey, V. S. Finn, J. J. Gill, S.J., *Affectivity and Sexuality: their Relationship to the Spiritual and Apostolic Life of Jesuits. Comments on Three Experiences* (Studies X, 2–3: March-May, 1978).

W. C. Spohn, S. J., *St. Paul on Apostolic Celibacy* (Studies XVII, 1: January, 1985).

J. A. Tetlow, S. J., *A Dialogue on the Sexual Maturing of Celibates* (Studies XVII, 3: May, 1985).

V. Fourth Week of Lent: JESUIT POVERTY

1. Sunday, Fourth Week of Lent

If one is pleased to remain in the Society, his food, drink, clothing, shoes and lodging will be what is characteristic of the poor; and he should persuade himself that it will be what is worst in the house, for his greater abnegation and spiritual progress and to arrive at a certain equality and common norm among all. For where the Society's first members have passed through these necessities and greater bodily wants, the others who come to it should endeavor, as far as they can, to reach the same point as the earlier ones, or to go farther in our Lord.

(*General Examen* [81] 26: Ganss 100)

2. Monday, Fourth Week of Lent

All who are under the obedience of the Society should remember that they ought to give gratuitously what they have gratuitously received (Matt. 10.9), without demanding or accepting any stipend or alms in recompense for Masses or confessions or preaching or lecturing or visiting or any other ministry among those which the Society may exercise according to our Institute, that thus it may proceed in the divine service with greater liberty and greater edification of the neighbor.

(*Constitutions* VI, 2 [565] 7: Ganss 256)

3. Tuesday, Fourth Week of Lent

No matter how hard it may happen to be, holy poverty should be accepted voluntarily. But really it is not hard; rather, it is the cause of great delight in one who embraces it willingly... If this is true of people who are not poor by choice, what shall we say of those who are poor because they choose to be? For, neither possessing nor loving anything earthly which they could lose, they enjoy a peace that is imperturbable and a tranquillity that is supreme. On the other hand, riches are for those who possess them like the sea that is tossed by the storm. Moreover, these voluntary poor, because of the peace and security of their conscience, enjoy an uninterrupted cheerfulness which is like a banquet without end...

I will add only this, that those who love poverty should, as occasion offers, love her retinue, which consists of poor meals, poor clothes, poor sleeping accommodations, and to be held of little account. Whoever loves poverty and is unwilling to feel want, or any of its effects, would be a very dainty poor man and would give the impression of one who loved the name rather than the reality, of one who loved rather in words than in the depth of his heart.

(St. Ignatius Loyola [Juan Polánco], Letter to the Members of the Society in Padua [August 7, 1547]: Young 149f.)

4. Wednesday, Fourth Week of Lent

Our poverty in the Society is apostolic: our Lord has sent us "to preach in poverty". Therefore our poverty is measured by our apostolic end, so that our entire apostolate is informed with the spirit of poverty...

Our poverty should become a sign of our charity in that by our lack we enrich others. Nothing should be our own, so that all things may be common in Christ. Communities themselves, renouncing their own advantage, should be united to each other by the bond of solidarity. Finally, the parts of the Society should freely become poorer, so that they may serve the whole body of the Society. And the bond of charity should not be restricted only to Jesuits, for all people are related to the Mystical Body of Christ. Charity should always crown the obligations of justice, by which we are bound in a special way to those who are poorer and to the common good.

(G.C. 31, 288, 295: *Poverty* [Decree 11], pars. 4, 9)

5. Thursday, Fourth Week of Lent

The Society cannot meet the demands of today's apostolate without reform of its practice of poverty. Jesuits will be unable to hear the "cry of the poor" (Ps. 9.13; Job 34.28; Prov. 21.13) unless they have greater personal experience of the miseries and distress of the poor. It will be difficult for the Society everywhere to forward effectively the cause of justice and human dignity if the greater part of her ministry identifies her with the rich and powerful, or is based on the "security of possession, knowledge and power" (Paul VI, *Evangelica Testificatio* 19). Our life will be no "witness to a new and eternal life won by Christ's redemption or to a resurrected state and the glory of the heavenly kingdom" (*Lumen Gentium* 44), if, individually or corporately, Jesuits are seen to be attached to earthly things, even apostolic institutions, and to be dependent on them. Our communities will have no meaning or sign value for our times, unless, by their sharing of themselves and all they possess, they are clearly seen to be communities of charity and of concern for each other and all others.

(G. C. 32, 261: *Poverty* [Decree 12], par. 5)

6. Friday, Fourth Week of Lent

Christ asks only that we open our heart to him in all simplicity, in the acknowledgement of our own poverty and misery, to obtain from him the gift of our conversion to him, which we all need if we are to share in the joy of his Kingdom. St. Ignatius of Loyola explains this point by saying that poverty is the first step to be taken to share in the Kingdom of Christ, by following him, imitating his style, and so attaining liberation.

For this is an enriching poverty. Paradoxical as it may sound, the poorest who have freely opted for this poverty are the richest, for they have discovered the hidden treasure, which is authentic independence from things and chiefly from their own selves. This option for Christ poor—a Christ on the cross, naked and despised, who is waiting with open arms to liberate us—snatches from us our false hopes and idolatries. Things are no longer ends, little gods, but become means; our trust is placed in God alone, the source of peace and happiness. We adhere to that marvelous power which is at work on Calvary and contains the germ of the resurrection.

(Pedro Arrupe, S.J., "The Seven Words of the Living Christ" [1977] 2: *Justice* 214)

7. *Saturday, Fourth Week of Lent*

On the cross, Jesus, whose unique Person is divine and eternally generated by the Father, feels his human nature rent asunder and calls on the Father, by whom he feels abandoned. His poverty is so complete that he needs his Father's will in order to continue subsisting. His only possession is his radical dependence on the Father. His wealth is his poverty, since his subsistence is his dependence...

It is not surprising that in the *Exercises* poverty "both spiritual and actual" should be a pivotal point for determining the process of following Christ. For us Jesuits who have individually and collectively opted to follow Christ in a total way with "offerings of greater value and of more importance" (*Spir. Ex.* 97f.), this theological poverty must lead us, in fact, to actual poverty. In the light of this trinitarian poverty and total disappropriation, many of our religious catchwords in the area take on their full meaning: frugality, the standard of living of honest priests, the life that is that of the poor, solidarity with the poor. In that light, too, many of the sufferings of our day appear in all their poignant tragedy: the absolute dereliction of individuals and of whole peoples, the spiritual anguish of non-believers, the moral misery of those who deny by their day-to-day lives what they believe in the depths of their hearts. The Lord who redeemed us in poverty can be helped only in poverty and from poverty.

(Pedro Arrupe, S.J., "The Trinitarian Inspiration of the Ignatian Charism" [1980] 93, 95: *Legacy* 130ff.)

Recommended for Further Reading:

Constitutions VI, c. 2.

St. Ignatius Loyola, Letter to Jaime Cazador (February 12, 1536), Young 13–18.

—, Letter to the Members of the Society in Padua (August 7, 1547), Young 146–150.

—, *Spiritual Diary*.

G. C. 31, *Poverty* (Decree 18).

G. C. 32, *Poverty* (Decree 12).

Pedro Arrupe, S.J., "On Poverty, Work and the Common Life" (1968), *Planet* 143–163; *Challenge* 11–34.

—, "Some Reflections on the Practice of Poverty" (1973), *Challenge* 95–100.

—, "Simplicity of Life" (1973), *Planet* 165–181; *Challenge* 113–130.

D. B. Knight, S.J., *St. Ignatius' Ideal of Poverty* (Studies IV, 1: January, 1972).

H. de la Costa, S.J., E. Sheridan, S.J., *et al.*, *On Becoming Poor. Symposium on Evangelical Poverty* (Studies VIII, 2–3: March–May, 1976).

J. A Tetlow, S.J., *The Transformation of Jesuit Poverty* (Studies XVIII, 5: November, 1986).

VI. Fifth Week of Lent: JESUIT OBEDIENCE

1. Sunday, Fifth Week of Lent

To make progress, it is very expedient and highly necessary that all should devote themselves to complete obedience, by recognizing the superior, whoever he is, as being in the place of Christ our Lord and by maintaining interior reverence and love for him. They should obey entirely and promptly, not only by exterior execution of what the superior commands, with becoming energy and humility, and without excuses and murmurings even though things are commanded which are difficult and repugnant to sensitive nature; but they should try to maintain in their inmost souls genuine resignation and true abnegation of their own wills and judgments, by bringing their wills and judgments wholly into conformity with what the superior wills and judges, in all things in which no sin is seen, and by regarding the superior's will and judgment as the rule of their own, in order to conform themselves more completely to the first and supreme rule of all good will and judgment, which is the Eternal Goodness and Wisdom.

(*Constitutions* III, 1 [284] 23: Ganss 164)

2. Monday, Fifth Week of Lent

For this (i.e., the preservation of the true spirit of the Society) it will be very useful if the scholastics and others among its members be very well trained in obedience. It should make no difference to them who the superior is, but they should recognize Christ our Lord in each of their superiors and be careful to obey him in his representative. The reason for this advantage is that, while this virtue of obedience is very necessary for every congregation, it is especially so in this Society, which is made up of highly educated men, some of whom are sent on im-

39

portant missions by the pope and other prelates, others scattered in remote places far from any superior, associating with great personages—and for many other reasons. Now, if their obedience is not of a very high quality, such men could hardly be ruled at all. And therefore I hold that there is no duty more opportune and necessary for the common good of the Society than a constant and careful obedience.

(St. Ignatius Loyola, Letter to the College of Gandía [July 29, 1547]: Young 144)

3. Tuesday, Fifth Week of Lent

We may allow ourselves to be surpassed by other religious orders in fasts, watchings, and other austerities, which each one, following its institute, holily observes. But in the purity and perfection of obedience, together with the true resignation of our wills and the abnegation of our judgment, I am very desirous, my dear brothers, that they who serve God in this Society should be conspicuous, so that by this virtue its true sons may be recognized as men who regard not the person whom they obey, but in him Christ our Lord, for whose sake they obey. For the superior is to be obeyed not because he is prudent, or good, or qualified by any other gift of God, but because he holds the place and the authority of God; as Eternal Truth has said: "He that hears you, hears me; and he that despises you, despises me" (Luke 10.16).

(St. Ignatius Loyola, Letter to the Members of the Society in Portugal ["Letter on Obedience"; March 26, 1553]: Young 288)

4. Wednesday, Fifth Week of Lent

Therefore, my dear brothers, try to make the surrender of your wills entire. Offer freely to God through his ministers the liberty he has bestowed on you. Do not think it a slight advantage of your free will [that you have] the ability of restoring it wholly in obedience to him who gave it to you. In this you do not lose it, but rather perfect it, in conforming your will wholly with the most certain rule of all rectitude, which is the divine will, the interpreter of which is the superior who governs you in place of God...

But anyone who aims at making an entire and perfect oblation of himself, in addition to his will, must offer his understanding, which is a further and the highest degree of obedience. He must not only will, but think the same as the superor, submitting his own judgment to the superior, so far as a devout will can bend the understanding. For while this faculty has not the freedom of the will, and naturally gives its assent to what is presented to it as true, there are, however, many instances where the evidence of the known truth is not coercive, and it can, with the help of the will, favor one side or the other. When this happens, every truly obedient man should conform his thought to the thought of the superior.

(St. Ignatius Loyola, Letter to the Members of the Society in Portugal ["Letter on Obedience"; March 26, 1553]: Young 290)

5. Thursday, Fifth Week of Lent

Obedience is the ordinary means by which God's will is made clear to the members of the Society. However, it does not take away, but rather by its very nature and perfection supposes in the subject the obligation of personal responsibility and the spirit of ever seeking what is better. Consequently the subject can, and sometimes should, set forth his own reasons and proposals to the superior. Such a way of acting is not opposed to perfect obedience, but is reasonably required by it, in order that by an effort common to both superior and subject the divine will may more easily and surely be found. For obedience of judgment does not mean that our intellect is bereft of its proper role, and that one should assent to the superior's will against reason, rejecting the evidence of truth. For the Jesuit, employing his own intelligence, confirmed by the unction of the Holy Spirit, makes his own the will and judgment of superiors, and with his intellect endeavors to see their orders as more conformed to the will of God...

Thus understood, obedience is not opposed to the dignity of the human person who obeys, nor to his maturity and liberty, but rather strengthens such liberty and admirably fosters the progress of the human person by purification of heart and assimilation to Christ and his mother.

(G. C. 31, 280f.: *The Life of Obedience* [Decree 17], pars. 11f.)

6. *Friday, Fifth Week of Lent*

Vowed obedience, whether in humdrum or in heroic matters, is always an act of faith and freedom whereby the religious recognizes and embraces the will of God, manifested to him by one who has authority to send him in the name of Christ. He does not necessarily have to understand why he is being sent. But both the superior who sends and the companion who is sent gain assurance that the mission is really God's will if it is preceded by the dialogue that is the account of conscience. For by it, the superior acquires an inner knowledge of those subject to his authority: what they can and what they cannot do, and what help they need by way of counsel or resource to do what they can. The companion, in turn, learns what the mission on which he is being sent involves, and what, concretely, he must do to discharge his responsibility.

The more the account of conscience is genuinely practiced, the more authentic will our discernment be of God's purpose in our regard and the more perfect that union of minds and hearts from which our apostolate derives its dynamism.

(G. C. 32, 231f.: *The Union of Minds and Hearts* [Decree 11], pars. 31f.)

7. *Saturday, Fifth Week of Lent*

In obedience there is the very essence of the imitation of Christ, "who redeemed by obedience the world lost by its lack, *factus obediens usque ad mortem, mortem autem crucis"* (St. Ignatius Loyola, Letter on Obedience [Young 288]). In obedience lies the secret of apostolic fruitfulness. The more you do the works of pioneers, the more you need to be closely united with him who sends you: "All apostolic boldness is possible, when the apostles' obedience is certain " (Loew, *Journal d'une mission ouvrière,* p. 452). We are certainly aware that if obedience demands much from those who obey, it demands even more of those who exercise authority. The latter are required to listen without partiality to the voices of all of their sons, to surround themselves with prudent counsellors in order to evaluate situations sincerely, to choose before God what best corresponds to his will and to intervene with firmness whenever there is departure from that will. In fact, every son or daughter of the Church is well aware that obedience is the proof and foundation of fidelity.

(Pope Paul VI, Address to the Members of G. C. 32 [December 3, 1974]: *Documents of the 31st and 32nd General Congregations of the Society of Jesus* [St. Louis, 1977], p. 535)

44

Recommended for Further Reading:
Constitutions, VI, c. 1.
St. Ignatius Loyola, Letter to the College of Gandía (July 29, 1547), Young 140–146.
—, Letter to the Community at Coimbra (January 14, 1548), Young 159–162.
—, Letter to Fr. Andrés Oviedo (March 27, 1548), Young 164–172.
—, Letter to the Members of the Society in Portugal ("Letter on Obedience"; March 26, 1553), Young 287–295.
—, Instructions on the Method of Dealing with Superiors (December 1, 1554), Young 390–392.
G. C. 31, *The Life of Obedience* (Decree 17).
T. H. O'Gorman, S.J., *Jesuit Obedience: from Life to Law* (Manila, 1971).
D. B. Knight, S.J., *Joy and Judgment in Religious Obedience* (Studies VI, 3: April, 1974).
J. J. Gill, S.J., *A Jesuit's Account of Conscience—for Personal and Organizational Effectiveness* (Studies IX, 5: November, 1977).
R. F. Harvanek, S.J., *The Status of Obedience in the Society of Jesus* (Studies X, 4: September, 1978).
I. de la Potterie, S.J., G. Pelland, S.J., T. Špidlik, S.J., G. Dumeige, S.J., M. Gioia, S.J., J.-Y. Calvez, S.J., H. Rahner, S.J., *Looking at All Three Together. Obedience: Christian, Religious, Jesuit* (CIS 31: X, 2 [1979]).

VII. Holy Week: THE WAY OF JESUS

1. *Sunday of the Passion*

Just as the people of the world, who follow the world, love and seek with such great diligence honors, fame, and esteem for a great name on earth, as the world teaches them, so those who are progressing in the spiritual life and truly following Christ our Lord love and intensely desire everything opposite. That is to say, they desire to clothe themselves with the same clothing and uniform of their Lord, because of the love and reverence which he deserves, to such an extent that where there would be no offense to his Divine Majesty and no imputation of sin to the neighbor, they would wish to suffer injuries, false accusations, and affronts, and to be held and esteemed as fools (but without their giving any occasion for this), because of their desire to resemble and imitate in some manner our Creator and Lord Jesus Christ, by putting on his clothing and uniform, since it was for our spiritual profit that he clothed himself as he did. For he gave us an example that in all things possible to us we might seek, through the aid of his grace, to imitate and follow him, since he is the way which leads us to life.

(*General Examen* [101] 44: Ganss 107f.)

2. *Monday of Holy Week*

We desire to know only Christ Jesus who, sent forth from the Father, consummated the work of saving creation by his life, death, and resurrection. Risen now and exalted by the Father, he draws all things to himself through the Holy Spirit, whom he has sent into the world, so that in him all may be one as he and the Father are one. Thus, through the grace of our vocation, at once both religious and apostolic, we share in the salvific work of Christ, partaking more fully and intimately of Christ's own love for the Father and for all people, for he loved us unto the end and gave himself as a ransom for all. Here, then, is our vocation: to love the Father and his children, to work with Christ in his Church for the life of the world that the Father may receive greater glory, to strive towards our goal in the Spirit—this is the ever-flowing fount of the joy of our charity and the offering of our strength.

(G. C. 31, 211: *Prayer* [Decree 14], par. 2)

3. Tuesday of Holy Week

It is an essential trait of the Ignatian charism, and one of clear Trinitarian origin in the vision of La Storta, that the following of Christ is to be done in humiliation and the cross... The life of Ignatius, dotted with lawsuits and sentences—sometimes insistently demanded by Ignatius, since putting an end to accusations made him freer for greater service—taught him experientially that the following of Christ brings much hostility. With his habitual flair for reflection, he had seen that persecutions are lacking only when we do not work at our apostolate.

But the cross that the Lord bore on his shoulders means not only external persecutions; it also, and primarily, means following him in humility, poverty, self-abnegation. It means stripping oneself of everything, including honor and good name, regarding these as well sacrificed when "greater service" is at stake.

(Pedro Arrupe, S.J., "The Trinitarian Inspiration of the Ignatian Charism" [1980] 73f.: *Legacy* 121f.)

4. Wednesday of Holy Week

The rediscovery of what might be called the "social dimension" of the Eucharist is of tremendous significance today. We once again see Holy Communion as the Sacrament of our brotherhood and unity. We share in a meal together, eating the same bread from the same table. And St.Paul tells us clearly: "The fact that there is only one loaf means that, though there are many of us, we form a single body because we all have a share in this one loaf" (I Cor 10.17). In the Eucharist, in other words, we receive not only Christ, the Head of the Body, but its members as well.

This fact has immediate practical consequences, as St. Paul once again reminds us. "God has arranged the body so that... each part may be equally concerned for all the others. If one part is hurt, all parts are hurt with it" (I Cor 12,24–26). Wherever there is suffering in the body, wherever members of it are in want or oppressed, we, because we have received the same body and are part of it, must be directly involved. We cannot opt out or say to a brother or sister: "I do not need you. I will not help you."

(Pedro Arrupe, S.J., "Eucharist and Hunger" [1976] 3: *Justice* 176f.)

5. Holy Thursday

The central ideal which your movement presents to you is that of a "man of the Eucharist," that is, of a man who, like Jesus, carries to the very end the plan of the Father, dedicating himself totally to others, letting his heart be broken for them on a universal level open to all the world, to all people. This man of the Eucharist is the new man, the man who wishes to build a new world with Jesus...

True "men of the Eucharist," who are engaged in building a new world, are those who follow their Lord wherever he goes and who, to follow him, are nourished by his Body and Blood, and are thus transformed into "other Christs"..., on fire with the love of Christ, who is the only one who can transform the egoism of the heart of stone of the "old man" in the men and women of today.

(Pedro Arrupe, S.J., "The Eucharist and Youth": Address to Teenagers of the "Youths' Eucharistic Movement" [1979] 8: *Apostolates* 305, 307)

6. Good Friday

The death of Jesus was not an easy one. He did not die in bed, surrounded by the company of his disciples, quietly, as it became a great teacher. Jesus dies alone, to all indications a failure, even without the inner comfort from his Father, who has left him for a time that he may die a human death to the full. And in these moments, to teach us an object lesson of faith, Jesus consciously accepts death and throws himself into the only thing he knows is left to him, his Father's arms.

We know that our death, too, mine and yours, is a once-in-a-lifetime experience, in which no one can take our place. We shall die in complete solitude, even if exteriorly we are well accompanied. We have gone through a pale experience of this when we lost one of our dear ones; our very bones seem to shudder. At that time only faith brings comfort to the heart, that instinctively shrinks from the privation of life.

But to obtain this faith, at least a moment of interior conversion is required that may restore our consciousness of being creatures. It is only the little ones that know how to die well, those who, like Jesus, put all their trust in the Father, into whose embrace they are going to fall after the bitter draught of death.

(Pedro Arrupe, S. J., "The Seven Words of the Living Christ" [1977] 6: *Justice* 222f.)

7. Holy Saturday

The way of the cross of Christ continues, then, to open up for us the other way (to heal the effects of sin), that of participation in redemptive suffering. We will all meet it in our life, as he met it, however little we may feel ourselves honored to struggle with him against our own selfishness and that of others, and provided that we do not flee in a cowardly fashion when it knocks at our door...

It is necessary to struggle against injustice in the name of God and of humanity, since we are children of God, in the solidarity of the total Christ. But it is necessary also to continue to teach men and women that evil can be transformed into good through love, fidelity, sacrifice, and even death. Jesus of Nazareth was not a politician. But with his death on the cross and fidelity to his prophetic mission, concentrating against himself the forces of sin and of human selfishness, he vanquished them more effectively than by any political action, through his redemptive love and his example.

(Pedro Arrupe, S. J., "The Jesuit and the Christ of the Spiritual Exercises" [1971] 11: *Apostolates* 271f.)

50

Recommended for Further Reading:

Pedro Arrupe, S.J., "Eucharist and Hunger" (1976), *Justice* 171–181.

—, "The Seven Words of the Living Christ" (1977), *ibid.*, 209–225.

—, "The Jesuit and the Christ of the Spiritual Exercises" (1971), *Apostolates* 255–282.

—, "The Eucharist and Youth" (1979), *ibid.*, 283–307.

VIII. First Week of the Easter Season: SENT BY THE RISEN LORD

1. Easter Sunday

God is alive and more present than many imagine. The abandonment, the total solitude of Christ on the cross has yielded its fruit. It seemed as though our eyes could see only what is negative. But the power of the one crucified has set the earth on fire, and the Spirit is doing his work in each person's heart. We must cleanse our sleepy eyes and learn how to see. We shall be surprised, and we shall burst into an irrepressible shout of praise...

The Christian salvation of the human person is not merely a promise of a blissful beyond, but the reality of true brotherhood perfected in justice, as a real anticipation of the life to come. Christ died and rose that love may reign supreme in the world, and consequently also justice—thus he condemned egoism and injustice. In a word, he rose that God might in fact be the Father of all, in a universal brotherhood.

(Pedro Arrupe, S.J., "The Seven Words of the Living Christ" [1977] 4, 5: *Justice* 219f.)

2. Monday, First Week of Easter

The created humanity which became perverted and transformed into a sinful humanity, in which some people oppress others and prevent them from attaining integral development, is also the humanity re-created by Christ. This re-creation of humanity by Christ constitutes an essential element of the historic situation of humanity.

The Jesuit has as his only *raison d'être* his incorporation into the task of re-creating humanity with Christ. On the degree of his complete and existential participation in the spirit of Christ, the restorer of the human race, depends, more than on any other factor, the success of his mission in the history of the world's salvation.

(Pedro Arrupe, S.J., "The Social Commitment of the Society of Jesus" [1971] 24: *Justice* 52f.)

3. Tuesday, First Week of Easter

The only-begotten Son has been sent by the Father to save what was lost, and through the Holy Spirit to unite the men and women who were redeemed by him into one Mystical Body, which is the Church.

As the Son was sent by the Father, he in turn sent the apostles (John 20.21) as heralds of saving charity, giving them this solemn command: "Go, therefore, and make disciples of all nations, baptizing them... and behold, I am with you all days, even unto the consummation of the world" (Matt. 28. 19f.).

As part of the pilgrim Church, therefore, the Society has embraced as strongly as it can the Church's universal mission, and is so alive with this missionary spirit that it necessarily communicates to its members a zeal for souls great enough to make both the defense of the faith and its propagation one and the same vocation.

(G. C. 31, 415f., 420: *Mission Service* [Decree 24], pars. 1f.)

4. Wednesday, First Week of Easter

Since the goal to which the Society directly tends is "to help our own souls and the souls of our neighbor to attain the ultimate end for which they were created" (*Const.* [307]), it is necessary that our life—of priests as well as scholastics and brothers—be undividedly apostolic and religious. This intimate connection between the religious and apostolic aspects in the

Society ought to animate our whole way of living, praying and working, and impress on it an apostolic character.

(G. C. 31, 204: *Religious Life in General* [Decree 13], par. 3)

5. Thursday, First Week of Easter

Our Society was founded principally for the defense and propagation of the faith and for the rendering of any service in the Church that may be for the glory of God and the common good (*Formula Instituti* [3] [1]). In fact, the grace of Christ that enables and impels us to seek "the salvation and perfection of souls"—what might be called, in contemporary terms, the total and integral liberation of the human person, leading to participation in the life of God himself—is the same grace by which we are enabled and impelled to seek "our own salvation and perfection" (*General Examen* [3] 2)....

A Jesuit, therefore, is essentially a man on a mission: a mission which he receives immediately from the Holy Father and from his own religious superiors, but ultimately from Christ himself, the one sent by the Father (John 17.18). It is by being sent that the Jesuit becomes a companion of Jesus.

(G. C. 32, 21 and 24: *Jesuits Today* [Decree 2], pars. 11 and 14.)

6. Friday, First Week of Easter

As we implement our mission, the Exercises invite us to contemplate the world of today with the loving gaze of the three Divine Persons, that we may be drawn to understand its needs as God does, and offer ourselves to share in his work of its salvation. As expressed in the Institute, the mission of the Society consists in the integral salvation in Jesus Christ of all women and men, a salvation begun in the present life and brought to its fulfilment in the life to come. In this mission, the promotion of justice is today a matter of growing urgency in the Church's work of evangelization; this dimension of our apostolate must therefore be fostered with particular care.

(G. C. 33, 37: *Companions of Jesus Sent into Today's World* [Decree 1], par. 34)

7. *Saturday, First Week of Easter*

The Jesuit seeks not only to imitate Jesus Christ; he seeks also to *Christify* the world, to contribute, in the small measure of his powers and of the grace with which God calls him, to the realization of the plan of God, who wishes "to recapitulate all things in Christ" (Eph. 1.10)...

Our whole vision of things, of our possibilities and aspirations, ought to take account of this; otherwise, we will be fearful and lose courage in the face of a world which, after having felt itself immensely great and powerful by the unfolding of its science and technology, finds itself often helpless to realize love and justice. The believing Christian has the consciousness of being immensely strong, by the grace of God that lives in him, and capable of following the infinite example of love given him by the whole life of Jesus Christ.

And as we know by faith, grace is destined to culminate, after death and beyond all the bounds of human life, in the vision of God, in which finally will be revealed also what we are, in love without limits and without selfishness. God will be all in all, and we shall realize ourselves in him, the Total Christ attained in plenitude.

(Pedro Arrupe, S.J., "The Jesuit and the Christ of the Spiritual Exercises" [1971] 7: *Apostolates* 263f.)

Recommended for Further Reading:

G. C. 31, *Mission Service* [Decree 24].

Pedro Arrupe, S.J., "Apostolic Mission: Key to the Ignatian Charism" (1974), *Planet* 271–301.

B. J. F. Lonergan, S.J., *The Response of the Jesuit, as Priest and Apostle, in the Modern World* (Studies II, 3: September, 1970).

IX. Second Week of the Easter Season: SENT TO BUILD UP THE CHURCH

1. Second Sunday of the Easter Season

The vocation of Jesuits is a sort of brilliance shining forth from Christ: it fills them and moves them. From it is born a strong desire and determination to struggle for the salvation and perfection of souls, under obedience to the hierarchical Roman Church.

(Jerónimo Nadal, S.J., *Dialogue* 2.9.97 [*Mon. Nadal* V, 723]; quoted by Pedro Arrupe, S.J., "Our Way of Proceeding" 21 [1979]: *Legacy* 56)

2. Monday, Second Week of Easter

Whoever desires to serve as a soldier of God beneath the banner of the cross in our Society, which we desire to be designated by the name of Jesus, and to serve the Lord alone and the Church, his spouse, under the Roman pontiff, the vicar of Christ on earth, should, after a solemn vow of perpetual chastity, poverty, and obedience, keep what follows in mind. He is a member of a Society founded chiefly for this purpose: to strive especially for the defense and propagation of the faith and for the progress of souls in Christian life and doctrine...

(*Formula Instituti* [3] [1]: Ganss, p. 66)

3. Tuesday, Second Week of Easter

If we wish to proceed securely in all things, we must hold fast to the following principle: what seems to me white, I will believe black if the hierarchical Church so defines. For I must be convinced that in Christ our Lord, the bridegroom, and in his spouse, the Church, only one Spirit holds sway, which governs and rules for the salvation of souls. For it is by the same Spirit and Lord who gave the Ten Commandments that our holy Mother Church is ruled and governed.

(St. Ignatius Loyola, *Spiritual Exercises* 365: "Rules for Thinking with the Church" 13)

4. *Wednesday, Second Week of Easter*

Beyond the limits of the strict matter of our vow of obedience extends our duty of *thinking with the Church*. Our being united among ourselves depends, in the last analysis, on our being united in both mind and heart to the Church that Christ founded. The historical context in which St. Ignatius wrote his Rules for Thinking with the Church is, of course, different from ours. But there remains for us the one pillar and ground of truth, the Church of the living God (I Tim. 3.15), in which we are united by one faith and one baptism to the one Lord and to the Father (Eph. 4.5). It behooves us, then, to keep undimmed the spirit of the Ignatian rules and to apply them with vigor to the changed conditions of our times.

(G. C. 32, 233: *The Union of Minds and Hearts* [Decree 11], par. 33)

5. *Thursday, Second Week of Easter*

Love for the Church... takes in the entire Church, the whole people of God, both hierarchy and laity, and is a positive commitment of the whole person to building up the one Church of Christ. This love, which has always been part of our way of proceeding, takes concrete forms:

—It is a love made of openness and respect for every believer and for his faith. Especially for the faith of simple folk, serving them on their own level and accepting them with all the spontaneous manifestations of their popular religiosity.

—A love that means "keeping our minds ready and eager to give entire obedience" to our pastors, cooperating receptively and actively in their teaching.

—A love that implies our support of the research of those who cultivate the sacred sciences to enrich our understanding of revelation; and on a humbler level, this love impels us to give religious instruction even to "children and uneducated persons" (*Const.* [69, 528]).

—A love that makes us live, feel and suffer the Church's problems and limitations as our own, offering with the freedom and humility of the sons of God the charitable service of a constructive criticism that is, in effect, a self-criticism.

(Pedro Arrupe, S.J., "Our Way of Proceeding" [1979] 51: *Legacy* 76f.)

6. *Friday, Second Week of Easter*

Ignatius believes in the mystical unity of the Spirit with the Church, a unity which does not destroy the radical difference between the Spirit and the Church. And because of that belief Ignatius knows no other point of contact with the radical immediacy of God, and no other window onto what the Spirit of Christ sees, than the Church itself. This faith in the Spirit who raises up the Society for the Church, and this faith in the Church which recognizes in the Society the Spirit at work, could never, for Ignatius, be in contradiction to one another. For the Church of the Lord and the prophetic vocation of the Society on behalf of this Church are always of "the same Spirit" (*Spir. Ex.* 365).

For this reason we find among the first companions of Ignatius not an attitude of servile submission, but a spirit that is always constructive, always "building up the Church" in the Pauline sense. This spirit found expression in the service given unconditionally yet prudently, in a readiness to help that was at once loyal and sober, particularly in relation to the Vicar of Christ. Thus Father Polánco was able to write to Father Madrid: "If the members of the Society are papists, they are so in those matters in which they ought to be and in no others, and only in the interests of God's glory and the common good" (*Mon. Nadal* II, 263).

(Peter-Hans Kolvenbach, S.J., "The Society's Reception of the Thirty-third General Congregation" [1985] 20f.: *Legacy* 206f.)

7. Saturday, Second Week of Easter

Faithful to the desire of Ignatius to keep growing in communion with the Church, the General Congregation asks that the whole Society make an effort to "experience" the mystery of the Church and gain an interior understanding of the Church (cf. Decree I, 8)...

An ecclesial sense makes us understand how widespread an influence the Society can have in the "building up" of the Lord's Church. It reminds us also that no Jesuit is alone and no work of the Society is isolated in its activity. The quality of our apostolic life, the scientific competence of many Jesuits, and the trust which so many Jesuits and so many of our works inspire in the Church reflect back upon the whole of the apostolic body of the Society. But this apostolic cohesiveness characteristic of the Society also requires each individual to ponder his responsibility before the whole Society and for the Church, as he performs his ministry in word and in writing, whether as a minister of the Church's liturgy or as a citizen of his country. Each one involves all his companions, and the Society itself involves the Church, for better or for worse.

(Peter-Hans Kolvenbach, S.J., "The Society's Reception of the Thirty-third General Congregation" [1985] 22f.: *Legacy* 207f.)

Recommended for Further Reading:

Pope Paul VI, Address to the Members of the 32nd General Congregation (December 3, 1974): *Documents of the 31st and 32nd General Congregations of the Society of Jesus*, pp. 519–536.

Pedro Arrupe, S. J., "Ecclesial Service" (1978), *Challenge* 253–277.

J. H. Wright, S.J., G. Ganss, S.J., L. Orsy, S.J., *On Thinking with the Church Today* (Studies VII, 1: January, 1975).

V. O'Keefe, S.J., "Sentire cum Ecclesia," in *The Jesuits, towards G. C. XXXIII* (CIS 42: XIV, 2 [1983], 11–33).

M. Fois, S.J., C. de Dalmases, S.J., L. Gonzales, S.J., F. A. Pastor, S.J., G. O'Collins, S.J., P. Dezza, S.J., *"Sentire cum Ecclesia": History, Challenge Today, Pedagogy* (CIS 43: XIV, 3 [1983]).

X. Third Week of the Easter Season: SENT INTO THE WHOLE WORLD

1. Sunday, Third Week of Easter

The aim and end of this Society is, by traveling through the various regons of the world at the order of the supreme vicar of Christ our Lord or of the superior of the Society itself, to preach, hear confessions, and use all the other means it can with the grace of God to help souls.

(*Constitutions* IV [308]: Ganss 172)

2. Monday, Third Week of Easter

The intention of the fourth vow pertaining to the pope was not to designate a particular place but to have the members distributed throughout the various parts of the world. For those who first united to form the Society were from different provinces and realms and did not know into which regions they were to go, whether among the faithful or the unbelievers; and therefore, to avoid erring in the path of the Lord, they made that promise or vow in order that his Holiness might distribute them for greater glory to God. They did this in conformity with their intention to travel throughout the world and, when they could not find the desired spiritual fruit in one region, to pass on to another and another, ever intent on seeking the greater glory of God our Lord and the greater aid of souls.

(*Constitutions* VII, 1 [605]: Ganss 268)

3. Tuesday, Third Week of Easter

There are in this Order various kinds of person, and also various places where these persons live and engage in their activities... The places are distinguished as follows: houses of probation, colleges, houses of the professed, and journeys (*per-egrinationes*) or places where they are sent by command, for the purpose of ministry... The final place is the most glorious and ample, for there men are not called that they might help souls only from their houses; their special interest and goal is to seek out everywhere in the world those whom they might gain for Christ. Therefore, they ought always to be engaged in journeyings and missions, to whatever place either the supreme pontiff or their general might send them for the sake of ministry.

(Jerónimo Nadal, *Dialogue* 2.6.50, 52: *Mon. Nadal* V, 671, 673; partly tr. J. W. O'Malley, S.J., *To Travel to Any Part of the World: Jerónimo Nadal and the Jesuit Vocation* [Studies XVI, 2: March, 1984], 8)

4. *Wednesday, Third Week of Easter*

It was for the task of announcing the Gospel that God in his providence called, along with other heralds of the Gospel, our holy Father Ignatius and his companions. God set their hearts on fire with a zeal which made them desire at first to go to Jerusalem to help non-believers. And when this project proved impossible, this same zeal urged them to offer themselves without reservation to the vicar of Christ, so that he might show them what part of the Lord's vineyard stood most in need of their labors (*Const.* [618]).

And so the new-born Society, by this commitment to Christ's vicar, was established as an apostolic order for work "among believers and non-believers" (*Const.* [618]), and was made an intimate sharer in the mission mandate of the entire Church.

(G. C. 31, 418f.: *Mission Service* [Decree 24], par. 2)

5. *Thursday, Third Week of Easter*

The apostolic body of the Society to which we belong should not be thought of just in terms of the local community. We belong to a province, which should itself constitute an apostolic community in which discernment and coordination of the apostolate on a larger scale than at the local level can and should take place. Moreover, the province is part of the whole Society, which also forms one single apostolic body and community. It is at this level that the overall apostolic decisions and guidelines must be made and worked out, decisions and guidelines for which we should all feel jointly responsible.

This demands of all of us a high degree of availability and a real apostolic mobility in the service of the universal Church.

(G. C. 32, 117f.: *Our Mission Today* [Decree 4], pars. 68f.)

6. Friday, Third Week of Easter

We touch here the heart of our identity, the mark that should characterize us as followers of Jesus: namely, "to be available" (Hebr. 10. 7, 9). This is precisely the quality that impressed Ignatius as specific to the *Son* and therefore to the Jesuit who believes in the Son and is called to be conformed to his image in the world of today (Rom. 8.29).

Only with this thorough availability can we aspire and live up to the condition of "being sent" which guarantees our personal integration and true apostolic identity. With reason, therefore, Ignatian and Jesuit spirituality is focussed on this central objective: to form a man who is *available for mission*, truly "a new man".

(Pedro Arrupe, S.J., "Apostolic Availability" [1977]: *Challenge* 230; *Legacy* 12f.)

7. Saturday, Third Week of Easter

"What is the Society's purpose?" asks Nadal. And he gives the answer: "The greatest of all: the salvation and perfection of souls for the greater glory of God." (*Mon. Nadal* V, 52, n.33) "That is indeed the Society's only purpose: to strive for the greater glory of God in all things." (*ibid.* 199, n. 184)...

This purpose of the Society determines its way of proceeding. It opens worldwide possibilities for our apostolate; it puts a premium on our acceptance of the more difficult missions and, in consequence, calls for unlimited availability and mobility; it requires us to renounce any ministry involving a stability that would conflict with apostolic mobility, to forgo ecclesiastical dignities, to be limited by none of the restrictions on evangelizing activity that would affect mendicant or monastic congregations because of their traditional religious or community practices.

(Pedro Arrupe, S.J., "Our Way of Proceeding" [1979], 7f.: *Legacy* 48f.)

Recommended for Further Reading:

G. C. 31, *Mission Service* [Decree 24].

Pedro Arrupe, S.J., "Missionary Vocation and Apostolate" (1972), *Planet* 209–231; *Challenge* 55–77.

—, "Apostolic Availability" (1977), *Challenge* 226–238; *Legacy* 11–20.

—, Letter on Inculturation to the Whole Society (May 14, 1978), *Apostolates* 171–181.

J. W. O'Malley, S.J., *The Fourth Vow in its Ignatian Context* (Studies XV, 1: January, 1983).

—, *"To Travel to Any Part of the World"*: *Jerónimo Nadal and the Jesuit Vocation* (Studies XVI, 2: March, 1984).

B. E. Daley, S.J., *"In Ten Thousand Places"*: *Christian Universality and the Jesuit Mission* (Studies XVII, 2: March, 1985).

XI. Fourth Week of the Easter Season: THE SERVICE OF FAITH AND THE PROMOTION OF JUSTICE

1. Sunday, Fourth Week of Easter

What is it to be a companion of Jesus today? It is to engage, under the standard of the Cross, in the crucial struggle of our time: the struggle for faith and that struggle for justice which it includes.

(G. C. 32, 12: *Jesuits Today* [Decree 2], par. 2)

2. Monday, Fourth Week of Easter

Ignorance of the Gospel on the part of some, and rejection of it by others, are intimately related to the many grave injustices prevalent in the world today. Yet it is in the light of the Gospel that men and women will most clearly see that injustice springs from sin, personal and collective, and that it is made all the more oppressive by being built into economic, social, political, and cultural institutions of world-wide scope and overwhelming power.

Conversely, the prevalence of injustice in a world where the very survival of the human race depends on men and women caring for, and sharing with, one another is one of the principal obstacles to belief: belief in a God who is justice because he is love.

Thus the way to faith and the way to justice are inseparable ways.

(G. C. 32, 16–18: *Jesuits Today* [Decree 2], pars. 6–8)

3. Tuesday, Fourth Week of Easter

The service of faith and the promotion of justice cannot be for us simply one ministry among others. It must be the integrating factor of all our ministries; and not only of our ministries but of our inner life as individuals, as communities, and as a world-wide brotherhood. This is what our Congregation means by a decisive choice. It is the choice that underlies and determines all the other choices embodied in its declarations and directives.

(G. C. 32, 19: *Jesuits Today* [Decree 2], par. 9)

4. Wednesday, Fourth Week of Easter

Our service of faith and promotion of justice has made the Society confront the mystery of the Cross: some Jesuits have been exiled, imprisoned or put to death in their work of evangelization. Some have been prevented from attending this Congregation.

But we who engage in this mission are sinners. Our reading of Decree 4 of G. C. 32 has at times been "incomplete, slanted and unbalanced" (P. Arrupe, "Rooted and Grounded in Love" 67 [*Legacy* 185]). We have not always recognized that the social justice we are called to is part of that justice of the Gospel which is the embodiment of God's love and saving mercy (G.C. 32, Decr. 4, n. 18). We have not learned to enter fully into a mission which is not simply one ministry among others, but "the integrating factor of all our ministries" (G. C. 32, Decr. 2, n. 9). We have found it difficult to understand the Church's recent emphasis on changing the structures of society, and what our proper role should be in collaborating with the laity in this process of transformation.

(G. C. 33, 34f.: *Companions of Jesus Sent into Today's World* [Decree 1], pars. 31f.)

5. Thursday, Fourth Week of Easter

God calls us through Jesus Christ to be his children, and it is a call to a sublime liberty. But this higher liberty is in reality threatened and fettered by many slaveries of human origin. God wishes us free. The world and society should be the place where we can meet God in freedom. We are born capable of being free; our approach to freedom runs counter to a force aiming at conquest and domination. Human history has been the road of our progressive liberation, though it has been marked constantly by false steps and by recessions. Today the hopes and the menaces are at their apex.

The Jesuit of today who knows how to read "the signs of the times" understands the message of history and discerns in its light the actual call of God. He understands the divine love for the tens of millions of men and women who struggle for their advancement and their liberation... He sees in the misery and the frustration which makes them slaves the clearest effect of the *mysterium iniquitatis* of which St. Paul speaks. Animated by this vision, he ought to wish to offer himself personally for this task, ready to enter combat with lucidity and with courage, along the lines of the "third degree of humility": desiring to resemble Jesus Christ more and to imitate him more.

(Pedro Arrupe, S.J., "The Social Commitment of the Society of Jesus" [1971] 5: *Justice* 33f.)

6. Friday, Fourth Week of Easter

The Jesuit, because of the bond which unites him to Christ prophet and priest, cannot, when faced with violence and revolution, follow another road or refer to other criteria than those chosen personally by Christ. He ought to be a permanent witness of the only love capable of creating between human beings the communion without which human and Christian love is impossible. He ought to bend every effort that his message may reach the free conscience of men and women, that they may free themselves from the personal sins which, of necessity, become objective in unjust structures and inhuman systems; for it is the same man or woman who is their author, and who maintains them.

(Pedro Arrupe, S.J., "The Social Commitment of the Society of Jesus" [1971] 16: *Justice* 46.)

7. *Saturday, Fourth Week of Easter*

The more the Church in its entirety really lives the mystery of Christ—true God and true man—the more the Church will know how to give its life for the life of the world, denouncing the malignant forces which deform our social life.

Consequently, to be a priest or religious of itself implies a radicalism greater than any definite socio-political option. The Jesuit, like Christ, has no mission to work in behalf of definite socio-political, cultural or economic structures, whose temporal autonomy ought to be respected. But like Christ he will have to proclaim unceasingly the human values and the human dimensions which must be respected by every conception and every construction of society. Such is his authentic and specific commitment in history and for the service of humanity, stemming from his priestly and religious mission.

(Pedro Arrupe, S.J., "The Social Commitment of the Society of Jesus"'" [1971] 17: *Justice* 47f.)

Recommended for Further Reading;

G. C. 32, *Our Mission Today* [Decree 4].

Pope Paul VI, *Evangelii Nuntiandi* (1975).

P. Arrupe, S.J., "The Social Commitment of the Society of Jesus" (1971), *Justice* 29–59.

—, "Witnessing to Justice in the World" (1972), *Planet* 33–73; *Justice* 78–120.

—, "Men for Others" (1973), *Planet* 95–108; *Justice* 122–138.

—, "Some Far-reaching Vistas of Decree 4 of G. C. 32" (1976), *Justice* 140–170.

—, "Faith and Justice as a Task for European Christians" (1976), *ibid.* 183–194.

T. E. Clarke, S.J., *Ignatian Spirituality and Social Consciousness;* L. Orsy, S.J., *Faith and Justice: Reflections* (Studies VII, 4: September, 1975).

W. J. Connolly, S.J., and P. Land, S.J., *Jesuit Spiritualities and the Struggle for Social Justice* (Studies IX, 4: September, 1977).

F. Ivern, S.J., *The Future of Faith and Justice: a Critical Review of Decree 4* (Studies XIV, 5: September, 1982).

XII. Fifth Week of the Easter Season: A
PREFERENTIAL LOVE FOR THE POOR

1. Sunday, Fifth Week of Easter

Consider the address which our Lord makes to his servants and friends whom he sends on this enterprise, recommending to them to seek to help all, first by attracting them to the highest spiritual poverty, and should it please the Divine Majesty, and should he deign to choose them for it, even to actual poverty. Secondly, they should lead them to a desire for insults and contempt, for from these springs humility.

Hence, there will be three steps: the first, poverty as opposed to riches; the second, insults or contempt as opposed to the honor of this world; the third, humility as opposed to pride. From these three steps, let them lead men and women to all other virtues.

(St. Ignatius Loyola, *Spiritual Exercises* 146)

2. Monday, Fifth Week of Easter

I call poverty a grace because it is a very special gift from God; as Scripture says, "Poverty and riches are from God" (Sir. 11.14). How much God loved it his only-begotten Son has shown us, who, coming down from the kingdom of heaven, chose to be born in poverty and to grow up in it. He loved it, not only in life, suffering hunger and thirst, without any place to lay his head (see Matt. 8.20; Lk. 9.58), but even in death, wishing to be despoiled of everything, even his clothing, and to be in want of everything, even of water in his thirst...

Christ likewise showed us the high esteem he had of poverty in the choice and employment of his friends, who lived in poverty, especially in the New Testament, beginning with his most holy Mother and his apostles, and continuing on with so many Christians through the course of the centuries right up to the present, vassals imitating their king, soldiers their captain, and members their head, Jesus Christ...

Our Lord so preferred the poor to the rich that he chose the entire college of his apostles from among the poor, to live and associate with them, to make them princes of his Church and set them up as judges of the twelve tribes of Israel...

Friendship with the poor makes us friends of the eternal King. Love of poverty makes kings even on earth—kings not of earth but of heaven.

(St. Ignatius Loyola [Juan Polánco], Letter to the Members of the Society in Padua [August 7, 1547]: Young 147f.)

3. Tuesday, Fifth Week of Easter

Solidarity with men and women who live a life of hardship and who are victims of oppression cannot be the choice of a few Jesuits only. It should be a characteristic of the life of all of us as individuals, and a characteristic of our communities and institutions, as well. Alterations are called for in our manner and style of living, so that the poverty to which we are vowed may identify us with the poor Christ, who identified himself with the deprived...

If we have the patience and the humility and the courage to walk with the poor, we will learn from what they have to teach us what we can do to help them.

(G. C. 32, 97, 99: *Our Mission Today* [Decree 4], pars. 48, 50)

4. Wednesday, Fifth Week of Easter

The validity of our mission will depend, to a large extent, on our solidarity with the poor. For though obedience sends us, it is poverty that makes us believable. So, together with many other religious congregations, we wish to make our own the Church's preferential option for the poor. This option is a decision to love the poor preferentially because there is a desire to heal the whole human family. Such love, like Christ's own, excludes no one, but neither does it excuse anyone from its demands. Directly or indirectly, this option should find some concrete expression in every Jesuit's life, in the orientation of our existing apostolic works, and in our choice of new ministries. "Only when we come to live out our consecration to the Kingdom in a communion that is for the poor, with the poor and against all forms of human poverty, material and spiritual, only then will the poor see that the gates of the Kingdom are open to them." (P.-H. Kolvenbach, Homily in St. Peter's Basilica, Oct. 15, 1983)

(G. C. 33, 52: *Companions of Jesus Sent into Today's World* [Decree 2], par. 48)

5. Thursday, Fifth Week of Easter

Just as to create the consumer society, one begins by creating and educating "homo consumens", its basic element, so in the same way, in order to create a just and balanced society with the possibility of survival, we have to begin creating "homo serviens", who has a sense of solidarity and of being a brother or sister to all. On one side we have "homo consumens": egocentric, egotistical, obsessed with *having* rather than with being, a slave of self-created needs, unsatisfied and envious, whose only moral principle is to pile up wealth. On the other side, in contrast, is "homo serviens", who has no desire for more possessions, but for more being, who seeks to develop a capacity for service to others in solidarity, with a modest sense of what is "sufficient". Our first obligation as religious will be to become "homines servientes" who live with what is sufficient.

(Pedro Arrupe, S.J., "A New Service to the World of Today," [1977] 2: *Challenge* 245)

6. Friday, Fifth Week of Easter

Justice, then—even justice based on law and on rights—is not everywhere and always enough. There are versions of justice that take no account of the concrete existential situation of the persons and conditions to which it is applied. There are kinds of justice that are a cover-up for vested interests. A justice, a law that demands too little, leaves the helpless or oppressed man or woman defenceless. So, too, a violent law, a violent justice that demands too much, can become a hangman's noose for everyone... This sort of justice is not what Christ came to bring to the world. By the law, we were all condemned. But the justice of Christ went beyond the law, motivated as it was by charity. This is the charity that among men and women must complement justice, making it a higher sort of justice. It is the only one that can go on, beyond mere justice, to the point of meeting the needs of the human race. For its scope, going beyond the slogans of "equality for all" and "to each according to his merits", reaches out "to each according to his needs", which is the only truly human and Christian norm. That higher form of justice, which is charity, will have a preferential care for the poor, the weak and the oppressed in the name of a strict right, that, without charity, could turn out to be a *summa iniuria*.

(Pedro Arrupe, SJ., "Rooted and Grounded in Love" [1981]: *Legacy* 181)

7. Saturday, Fifth Week of Easter

In keeping with its vocation, the Society takes as its own the preferential option for the poor. But in so doing it will have to pass through a period of apprenticeship and of genuine experimentation in all sectors of its apostolic activity. For the Society, like the Church, while wholeheartedly committing itself to justice in the service of faith, does not know as yet all the concrete consequences of this for pastoral ministry, for the educational sector and even for the social apostolate...

One thing is certain: the Society's solidarity with the poor has a specific character different from that of a political party, a labor union or a development organization. This is because our option looks to the poor person as one who does not live by bread alone...

The prayer of Ignatius to be placed with the Son, answered at La Storta, becomes the prayer of the Society to be placed with those who incarnate, in and for his Church, the predilection of Christ.

(Peter-Hans Kolvenbach, S.J., "The Society's Reception of the Thirty-third General Congregation" [1985] 11f.: *Legacy* 201f.)

Recommended for Further Reading:

St. Ignatius Loyola [Juan Polánco], Letter to the Members of the Society in Padua (August 7, 1547), Young 146–150.

Pedro Arrupe, S.J., "A New Service to the World of Today" (1977), *Challenge* 239–252.

—, "A Change of Attitude towards the Underprivileged" (1977), *Justice* 241–252.

Peter-Hans Kolvenbach, S.J., "The Spiritual Exercises and Preferential Love for the Poor," in *The Experience of G.C. 33* (CIS 45: XV, 1 [1984]), 77–90.

XIII. Sixth Week of the Easter Season: OUR ACTUAL MINISTRIES

1. Sunday, Sixth Week of Easter

Whoever desires to serve as a soldier of God beneath the banner of the cross in our Society... should, after a solemn vow of perpetual chastity, poverty and obedience, keep what follows in mind. He is a member of a Society founded chiefly for this purpose: to strive especially for the defense and propagation of the faith and for the progress of souls in Christian life and doctrine, by means of public preaching, lectures, and any other ministration whatsoever of the word of God, and further by means of the *Spiritual Exercises*, the education of children and unlettered persons in Christianity, and the spiritual consolation of Christ's faithful through hearing confessions and administering the other sacraments. Moreover, this Society should show itself no less useful in reconciling the estranged, in holily assisting and serving those who are found in prisons or hospitals, and indeed in performing any other works of charity, according to what will seem expedient for the glory of God and the common good.

(*Formula Instituti* [3] [1]: Ganss 66)

2. Monday, Sixth Week of Easter

In short, our mission today is to preach Jesus Christ and to make him known in such a way that all men and women are able to recognize him whose delight, from the beginning, has been to be "with the sons of men" and to take an active part in their history (see Prov. 8.22-31; Col. 1.15-20).

(G. C. 32, 60: *Our Mission Today* [Decree 4], par. 11)

81

3. Tuesday, Sixth Week of Easter

The mandate of resisting atheism should permeate all the accepted forms of our apostolate, so that we may cultivate among believers true faith and an authentic awareness of God...

Jesuits should approach atheists with the firm conviction that the divine law is written in the hearts of all people, and with the belief that the Holy Spirit moves all people to the service they owe to God their creator. Both by a style of proclamation adapted to each person, combined with religious respect, and by a brotherly witness borne in the concrete details of living and acting, Jesuits should work to remove obstacles and to help atheists find and acknowledge God.

(G. C. 31, 34, 39: *The Task of the Society Regarding Atheism* [Decree 3], pars. 11, 16)

4. Wednesday, Sixth Week of Easter

An extensive and sincere collaboration with the laity is likewise to be commended. For in the works of our Society, our own responsibility for their inspiration, orientation and direction must be shared in a certain definite way by the laity. In the expanse, moreover, of the whole Church, serious care must be fostered to help the laity to grow and become true human beings and Christians, fully conscious of their own responsibility toward the Church and the world. This is especially true of those lay persons—men and women—who, because of their greater importance for the universal good of the Church, deserve special spiritual attention.

(G. C. 31, 373: *The Better Choice and Promotion of Ministries* [Decree 21], par. 9)

5. Thursday, Sixth Week of Easter: Ascension Thursday

Of great importance among the ministries of the Society are the educational and intellectual apostolates. Jesuits who work in schools of whatever kind or level, or who are engaged in non-formal or popular education, can exercise a deep and lasting influence on individuals and on society. When carried out in the light of our mission today, their efforts contribute vitally to "the total and integral liberation of the human person, leading to participation in the life of God himself." (G.C. 32, Decr. 2, par. 11) Research in theology and philosophy, in the other sciences and in every branch of human culture is likewise essential if Jesuits are to help the Church understand the contemporary world and speak to it the Word of Salvation. The opportunities and responsibilities of these apostolates require a change of heart and an openness to human needs around us; they also demand a solid intellectual formation. Jesuits in these fields and our men in more direct social and pastoral ministries should cooperate and benefit from one another's expertise and experience. Finally, the Society should promote the apostolate of the social communications media, which, like education and intellectual work, reaches large numbers of people and so permits "a more universal service to humanity" (G.C. 32, Decr. 4, par. 59).

(G. C. 33, 47: *Companions of Jesus Sent into Today's World* [Decree 1], par. 44)

6. Friday, Sixth Week of Easter

The Church is now engaged in a massive effort to educate—or rather to re-educate—herself, her children and all people so that we may all "lead our life in its entirety... in accord with the evangelical principles of personal and social morality to be expressed in a living Christian witness." (Synod of Bishops, 1971, *Justice in the World*, nn. 6, 37)

Today our prime educational objective must be to form men-
for-others: men and women who will live not for themselves
but for God and his Christ—for the God-man who lived and
died for all the world; men and women who cannot even con-
ceive of love of God which does not include love for the least
of their neighbors; men and women completely convinced that
love of God which does not issue in justice for their fellow
human beings is a farce.

(Pedro Arrupe, S.J., "Men for Others" [1973]: *Justice* 124)

7. *Saturday, Sixth Week of Easter*

Among new needs and situations we list, without any at-
tempt to be exhaustive, certain problems that call for our special
concern... While a number of Jesuits have already been working
for years in these areas, the General Congregation now wishes
to bring them to the attention of the whole Society:
—the spiritual hunger of so many, particularly the young, who
search for meaning and values in a technological culture;
—attacks by governments on human rights through assassi-
nation, imprisonment, torture, the denial of religious freedom
and political expression;
—the sad plight of millions of refugees searching for a permanent home;
—discrimination against whole categories of human beings,
such as migrants and racial or religious minorities;
—the unjust treatment and exploitation of women;
—public policies and social attitudes which threaten human life
for the unborn, the handicapped and the aged;
—economic oppression and spiritual needs of the unemployed,
of poor and landless peasants, and of workers, with whom
many Jesuits, like our worker priests, have identified themselves in order to bring them the Good News.

As an international body, the Society of Jesus commits itself
to that work which is the promotion of a more just world order,

greater solidarity of rich countries with poor, and a lasting peace based on human rights and freedom.

(G. C. 33, 48f.: *Companions of Jesus Sent into Today's World* [Decree 1], pars. 45f.)

Recommended for Further Reading:

St. Ignatius Loyola, Instruction to the Fathers at the Council of Trent (Spring, 1546), Young 94ff.

—, Letter to Fr. Diego Laynez (May 21, 1547), Young 132–137.

—, Instruction to the Fathers Sent to Germany (Sept. 24, 1549), Young 212ff.

Pedro Arrupe, S.J., "Jesuits and Racism" (1967), *Planet* 183–195.

—, "Jesuits and Ecumenism" (1971), *ibid.* 197–207.

—, "Progress Report on Jesuit Apostolates" (1978), *Apostolates* 25–31.

—, "Theological Reflection and Interdisciplinary Research" (1972), *ibid.* 33–42.

—, "Our Secondary Schools: Today and Tomorrow" (1980), *ibid.* 54–78.

—, "The Jesuit Mission in the University Apostolate" (1975), *ibid.* 79–95.

—, "The Intellectual Apostolate in the Society's Mission" (1976), *ibid.* 110–126.

—, "Mission among the Workers" (1980), *ibid.* 309–321.

—, "Rooted and Grounded in Love" (1981), *Legacy* 145–195.

Pope John Paul II, Allocution to Jesuit Curia and Provincials (February 27, 1982), *Acta Romana S.J.* 18 (1982), 721–735 (English trans. published by CIS).

M. Buckley, S.J., *Jesuit Priesthood: Meaning and Commitments* (Studies VIII, 5: December, 1976).

D. J. O'Brien, *The Jesuits and Catholic Higher Education* (Studies XIII, 5 (November, 1981).

J. Tetlow, S.J., *The Jesuits' Mission in Higher Education: Perspectives and Contexts* (Studies XV, 5: November, 1983-January, 1984).

W. C. Spohn, S.J., J. A. Coleman, S.J., T. E. Clarke, S.J., P.J. Henriot, S.J., *Jesuits and Peacemaking* (Studies XVII, 4: September, 1985).

A. Manaranche, S.J., "The Priestly Ministry in the Society of Jesus," in *Some Theological Aspects of Ignatian Spirituality* (CIS 48: XVI, 1 [1985]).

C. J. Beirne, S.J., *Compass and Catalyst: the Ministry of Administration* (Studies XVIII, 2: March, 1986).

XIV. SEVENTH WEEK OF THE EASTER SEASON: DISCERNING OUR WAY

1. Sunday, Seventh Week of Easter

To proceed more successfully in this sending of subjects to one place or another, one should keep the greater service of God and the more universal good before his eyes as the norm to hold oneself on the right course. It appears that in the vineyard of the Lord, which is so extensive, the following procedure of selection ought to be used. When other considerations are equal (and this should be understood in everything that follows), that part of the vineyard ought to be chosen which has greater need, because of the lack of other workers or because of the misery and weakness of one's fellow men and women in it and the danger of their eternal condemnation.

(*Constitutions* VII, 2 [622 a]: Ganss 274)

2. Monday, Seventh Week of Easter

Nothing that charity can do to help the neighbor is excluded from our Institute, provided that all our service is seen to be spiritual, and that we are quite clear on the point that the service proper to us is the more perfect one, namely, the purely spiritual ministries. We should not take up others that are in themselves lower except through necessity, after having given much thought to the question, with much hope and great fruit, and with the permission of Superiors; and finally, when service in the purely spiritual field is not feasible.

(Jerónimo Nadal, *Annotationes in Examen Generale: Mon. Nadal, Comm. de Inst.* 141.20; quoted by P. Arrupe, S.J., "Rooted and Grounded in Love" 35 [*Legacy* 165].)

3. Tuesday, Seventh Week of Easter.

The Jesuit community is a community of discernment. The missions on which Jesuits are sent, whether corporately or individually, do not exempt us from the need of discerning together in what manner and by what means such missions are to be accomplished. That is why we open our minds and hearts to our superiors and our superiors, in turn, take part in the discernment of our communities, always on the shared understanding that final decisions belong to those who have the burden of authority.

(G. C. 32, 29: *Jesuits Today* [Decree 2], par. 19)

4. Wednesday, Seventh Week of Easter

There are prerequisites for a valid communitarian discernment. On the part of the individual member of the community, a certain familiarity with the Ignatian rules for the discernment of spirits, derived from actual use; a determined resolution to find the will of God for the community, whatever it may cost; and, in general, the dispositions of mind and heart called for and cultivated in the First and Second Weeks of the *Exercises*. On the part of the community as such, a clear definition of the matter to be discerned, sufficient information regarding it, and "a capacity to convey to one another what each one really thinks and feels" (P. Arrupe, "De spirituali discretione," *Acta Romana S.J.* 15 [1971] 767-73)...

What is the role of the superior in communitarian discernment? It is, first, to develop, as far as he can, the requisite disposition for it; second, to decide when to convoke the community for it, and clearly to define its object; third, to take active part in it as the bond of union within the community and as the link between the community and the Society as a whole; and, finally, to make the final decision in the light of the discernment, but freely, as the one to whom both the grace and the burden of authority are given.

(G. C. 32, 220, 222: *The Union of Minds and Hearts* [Decree 11], pars. 22, 24)

5. *Thursday, Seventh Week of Easter*

It goes without saying that the involvement of everyone in searching for the will of God seems more appropriate at a time when the complexity of situations renders more difficult the analysis of their various aspects. Thus, to the need for participation is added the necessity, for the analysis of complex situations, of having recourse to every inspiration, human and spiritual, which the members of a community can bring. On the other hand, if everyone has been involved in the preparation of apostolic decisions, everyone is in a position to appropriate better those decisions which are taken. In any case, it should be clear that, far from limiting the exercise of authority and willingness to obey, the practice of discernment in common does no more than prepare the decision to be made by a competent superior. It does this by offering him all the aids of light, reflection, and prayer which can help him arrive more expeditiously at the will of God "here and now".

(Peter-Hans Kolvenbach, S.J., "On Apostolic Discernment in Common" [November 5, 1986], par. 31)

6. *Friday, Seventh Week of Easter*

The Holy Spirit has played a very real part in the whole process of the Society's renewal.

Throughout my generalate—before, during and after the General Congregation—I have constantly tried, since it is a fundamental duty of my office, to be alert to the signs of the Spirit in the Society: in its members, its communities, its apostolic life. I am convinced it is the Spirit which is breathing a new life into the Society and helping it to renew its service to the Church according to that "interior law of charity and love which the Holy Spirit writes and engraves upon hearts" (*Constitutions* 134). We will therefore only renew our service effectively insofar as we are faithful to the Spirit.

(Pedro Arrupe, S.J., Final Address to the Congregation of Procurators [1978] 19: *Legacy* 30)

7. *Saturday, Seventh Week of Easter*

In the midst of my ordinary prayer, with no further thought of the election, offering or asking God our Lord that the oblation made be accepted by his Divine Majesty, I felt an abundance of devotion and tears, and later, making a colloquy with the Holy Spirit before saying his Mass, with the same devotion and tears, I thought I saw him, or felt him, in a dense brightness, or in the color of a flame of fire. Quite unusual, and with all this, I felt satisfied with the election I made.

Later, in order to examine and discuss the election I had made, I took out the reasons I had written down to examine them. I prayed to our Lady, and then to the Son and to the Father, to give me their Spirit to examine and distinguish... At this moment other lights came to me, namely, how the Son first sent the Apostles to preach in poverty, and afterwards, the Holy Spirit, giving his Spirit and the gift of tongues, confirmed them, and thus the Father and the Son sending the Holy Spirit, all three Persons confirmed the mission...

Not much later, as I was going out to say Mass, coming to the short prayer, I felt intense devotion and tears at realizing or beholding in a certain manner the Holy Spirit, and the election as something finished...

(St. Ignatius Loyola, *Spiritual Journal* 10 [February 11, 1544]: tr. Young, in S. Decloux, *Commentaries on the Letters and Spiritual Diary of St. Ignatius Loyola* 137f.)

Recommendations for Further Reading:

Constitutions VII, 2 [622–624]. Pedro Arrupe, S.J., "Our Four Apostolic Priorities" (1970), *Apostolates* 1–8.

—, "De spirituali discretione" (December 25, 1971), *Acta Romana S.J.* 15 (1971), 767–773.

—, "Spiritual Renewal" (1971), *Challenge* 41–50.

—, "Jesuits and Continual Spiritual Renewal" (Three Conferences Given to Members of G. C. 32; December, 1974), *Planet* 303–341.

—, "Our Way of Proceeding" (1979), *Legacy* 43–85.

J. C. Futrell, S.J., *Ignatian Discernment* (Studies II, 2: April, 1970).

J. J. Toner, S.J., *A Method for the Communal Discernment of God's Will* (Studies III, 4: September, 1971).

J. C. Futrell, S.J., *Communal Discernment: Reflections on Experience* (Studies IV, 5: November, 1972).

L. Orsy, S.J., *Towards a Theological Evaluation of Communal Discernment* (Studies V, 5: October, 1973).

P. Penning de Vries, S.J., J. C. Futrell, S.J., A. Lefrank, S.J., *Communal Discernment: New Trends* (CIS Subsidia 14: Rome, 1975).

J. F. Conwell, S.J., *The Kamikaze Factor: Choosing Jesuit Ministries* (Studies XI, 5: November, 1979).

XV. PENTECOST SUNDAY: CREATOR SPIRIT

The Society was not instituted by human means; and neither is it through them that it can be preserved and developed, but through the omnipotent hand of Christ, God and our Lord. Therefore in him alone must be placed the hope that he will preserve and carry forward what he deigned to begin for his service and praise and for the aid of souls.

(*Constitutions* X [812] 1: Ganss 331)

Prayer

Lord, I need your Spirit, that divine force that has transformed so many human personalities, making them capable of extraordinary deeds and extraordinary lives. Give me that Spirit which, coming from you and going to you, infinite holiness, is a Holy Spirit...

Give me that Spirit that scrutinizes all, inspires all, teaches all, that will strengthen me to support what I am not able to support. Give me that Spirit that transformed the weak Galilean fishermen into the columns of your Church and into apostles who gave, in the holocaust of their lives, the supreme testimony of their love for their brothers and sisters.

Thus this life-giving outpouring will be like a new creation, of hearts transformed, of a sensibility receptive to the voice of the Father, of a spontaneous fidelity to his word. Thus you will find us again faithful and you will not hide your face from us, because you will have poured your Spirit over us. Now I understand that in order to accomplish all this one needs a love like that of the Father, a love that intervenes personally. "You,

93

Yahweh, are our Father... why do you let us stray from your ways?.. Oh, that you would tear the heavens open and come down!" (Is. 63,15-19)

Such was your definitive manifestation: the heavens open, a God the Father visible, a God the Son coming down to the earth and becoming human to save the world: "This mystery that has now been revealed through the Spirit to his holy apostles and prophets was unknown to any people in past generations..." (Eph. 3,5-14) This, then, is what I pray, kneeling before the Father: *Veni, Sancte Spiritus!*

"The one who guarantees these revelations repeats his promise: I shall indeed be with you soon. Amen; come, Lord Jesus. May the grace of the Lord be with you all. Amen." (Rev. 22.20f.)

(Pedro Arrupe, S.J., Final Address to the Congregation of Procurators [1978] 30: *Legacy* 40 ff.)

INDEX OF SOURCES USED

96